WIR
AN ANT

Also by GLADYS MARY COLES

POETRY

The Sounding Circle
Sinerva and Other Poems
The Snow Bird Sequence
Stoat, in Winter
Liverpool Folio
Studies in Stone
Leafburners: New and Selected Poems
The Glass Island
The Echoing Green

BIOGRAPHY AND CRITICISM

The Flower of Light: A Biography of Mary Webb
Introductions to Mary Webb's novels *Gone to Earth* and
    Precious Bane
Introduction to Mary Webb's essays *The Spring of Joy*
Mary Webb: a biographical study
Walks with Writers (with Gordon Dickins)
Mary Webb and Her Shropshire World

AS EDITOR

Both Sides of the River: Merseyside in Poetry & Prose
Poet's England: Lancashire
Poet's England: Cheshire
Mary Webb: Collected Prose and Poems
Selected Poems of Mary Webb
The Poet's View: Poems for Paintings in the Walker Art Gallery
The Life of Riley: A Selection from Joe Riley's Journalism

VIDEO

Secret Shropshire

Poet's England —— 22

Wirral
An Anthology

Compiled and Edited
by
GLADYS MARY COLES

HEADLAND

First published in 2002
by

HEADLAND PUBLICATIONS
38 York Avenue, West Kirby,
Wirral, CH48 3JF

A full CIP record for this book is available
from the British Library

ISBN 0 903074 73 7

HEADLAND acknowledges the financial
assistance of North West Arts Board
and the Metropolitan Borough of Wirral

---

*Printed in Great Britain by
L. Cocker & Co., Berry Street, Liverpool*

FOREWORD

The lovely Wirral Peninsula lies between two great rivers, the Dee and the Mersey, and is bordered on its northern coast by the Irish Sea. Truly it can be said that Wirral is defined by water. The Dee and the Mersey, contrasting in character, and the open Irish Sea, each have a pervasive and powerful influence on the peninsula and contribute considerably to its rich diversity of landscape and atmosphere.

Approximately fifteen miles long by seven in width, the Wirral Peninsula was once described in a picturesque metaphor as 'the spout of the tea-pot' (defining the shape of Cheshire). The topographical features repay closer description. Along its western coast, Wirral faces Wales across the wide Dee estuary, a wilderness teeming with birds where the ever-changing light enhances the mystery and beauty of the Welsh hills. An equally compelling scene is found along the parallel eastern coast of Wirral where the Mersey surges, broad and strongly tidal, an historically important river with a dramatic skyline of the city of Liverpool. Both rivers join the Irish Sea, constantly beating on Wirral's northern shore, often wild in winter and bringing the tang of brine on the wind.

I find all three of Wirral's coasts - and the alluring Hilbre Islands at the mouth of the Dee - a source of endless fascination and inspiration for my poems. Also Wirral's heartland of sandstone, heathery ridges and country lanes, its wildlife, its variety of towns and villages, its rich historical associations, offer a wealth of material for the poet. Researching the history and literature of Wirral for my earlier book *Both Sides of the River: Merseyside in Poetry and Prose,* I decided to compile a volume of poetry devoted to this unique peninsula and so began to gather my own poems on Wirral together with those of others.

It has proved a challenging and absorbing project compiling this, the first anthology to celebrate Wirral in poetry. My aim has been to evoke the peninsula's distinctive character and atmosphere, representing as many of its places, features and aspects as possible, its lively present and intriguing past, its culture and legends, old customs, such as Neston Ladies' Walking Day, and new ones, notably Thornton Hough's highly original Scarecrow Festival.

One of my primary intentions was to reflect in the anthology some facets of Wirral's interesting history: for instance, the influx of Romans, Anglo-Saxons and Viking Norse; and its maritime heritage, from the medieval 'ferry across the Mersey' to today's impressive 'Historic Warships' collection. It was important, too, to depict fine buildings such as Birkenhead Priory (12th century), Hamilton Square (1847), the magnificent Lady Lever Gallery (1922) and Port Sunlight 'garden village' (founded by Lever in 1888). Another of my aims was to highlight Birkenhead's achievements - the first street tramway system in Europe (1860), the first purpose-built public park in Britain (opened 1847, model for New York's Central Park), the first underwater railway tunnel in Europe (1886), the longest subaqueous tunnel in the world at the time of opening (the Mersey Tunnel, 1934). I also wanted to draw attention to some of the famous people who have lived here, such as Emma, Lady Hamilton, William Laird, Wilfred Owen, William Hesketh Lever (Viscount Leverhulme), Olaf Stapledon.

I have brought together poems from Anglo-Saxon times to the present day. The majority, though, are the work of contemporary poets, many of whom wrote their poems on specific subjects at my request for this anthology, often during the writing workshops and poetry courses I tutor for Liverpool University. Their work appears here alongside that of famous poets from the past such as Milton, Charles Kingsley, John Masefield and lesser-known 'local' names such as William Roscoe, Fred Bower (the 'Stonemason poet' of Heswall), John Pride and Roger Lancelyn Green.

The result is a unique collection, the 'Hundred of Wirral' (to use the old title) in the words of a hundred poets.

I need to emphasise that 'my' Wirral is this anthology equates to the historical and geographical entity which stretches from the Irish Sea coast to a southern boundary between Shotwick and Stanlow, entirely within Cheshire. The Wirral of my poetic tour ignores the 1974 Boundary Act which divided the peninsula, placing part in Merseyside and leaving the rest in Cheshire.

How have I arranged the poems? What direction does this poetic tour take?

The anthology begins in West Kirby and progresses along the Dee coast, darting inland at certain points to mid-Wirral and back, proceeding to Burton and Shotwick. From Shotwick, we travel directly across to the Mersey shore at Stanlow and Ellesmere Port. Then onward, with a little zig-zagging, to Port Sunlight and Birkenhead, following the Mersey to New Brighton. Turning here along the sea coast to Meols and Hoylake, we again move inland and back again, to arrive where we began, at West Kirby.

I have enjoyed enormously this task of creating a composite portrait of Wirral, capturing its essence in a rich tapestry of words and images. I hope the anthology will interest and delight readers familiar with Wirral, and entice those who are not to explore this historic peninsula 'betwixt the Mersey and the Dee'.

Gladys Mary Coles

CONTENTS

The Hundred of Wirral	*Gladys Mary Coles*	11
The Dee	*Dora Kennedy*	12
The Mersey	*John Masefield*	12
Old Rhyme	*Anon.*	14
from: Sir Gawain and the Green Knight	*(trans. J. R. Tolkien)*	14
The Shrine of St. Hildeburgh (Old Rhyme)	*Anon.*	14
From Hilbre Island	*Gladys Mary Coles*	15
Mr Blue	*John Curry*	16
Weather Rhyme	*Anon.*	16
Wet Spring Bank Holiday, Dee Estuary	*Gladys Mary Coles*	17
Whitsun West Kirby	*Dymphna Callery*	18
West Kirby Beach, New Year's Eve	*Carole Baldock*	19
Tell's Tower	*Peggy Poole*	20
On Hilbre	*Sue Craggs*	21
Takers (The Cockle War)	*Gladys Mary Coles*	22
Train Boys	*Philip Bastow*	24
A Child's Path	*Bruce Withers*	25
Thank You, Mr Stapledon	*J. M. Corfe*	26
A Window on the Wirral	*Carole Baldock*	26
Caldy	*Mary White*	27
Lines from Malta, 1917	*Frank Jocelyn Priest*	28
Haiku	*Linda Bradley*	28
The Wirral Way	*Mary Hodgson*	29
from: A January Walk	*Mary Brett*	30
Hillbark	*Mary White*	31
Thor's Stone	*Norma Jamieson*	33
Wirral Country Park Centre, Thurstaston	*Lindsay Coles*	34
Mancunians in the Dales	*Freda Rankin*	35
At the Highest Point, Poll Hill	*Miriam Bennett*	36
Heswall Beacons	*Kit Jackson*	37
from: The Pirate of Park West	*Fred Bower*	37
Sunset over the Dee	*Patricia Minter*	38
Heswall Days	*Martin Bennett*	38
Lower Village, Heswall	*Jane Brassey*	39
Remembrance Day, Heswall Lower Village	*Jacqui Baker*	40
The Dee Shore at Heswall	*John Pride*	41
from: Gayton Wake, 1804	*Richard Llwyd*	42
from: Lycidas	*John Milton*	44
Spring Tide in the Dee Estuary	*Dora Kennedy*	45
Emma Lyon	*John Pride*	46
Ashfield Hall Farm	*Lorna Home*	47
To a Sculptured Head	*Dora Kennedy*	48
Almond Trees at Clatterbridge, 1995	*Freda Rankin*	48
Mid-Wirral Lanes, Autumn Ride	*Ceri Courtenay*	49
Thornton Hough	*Betty Hodges*	49
Scarecrow Festival, Thornton Hough	*Ceri Courtenay*	51
Almost an Encounter (Raby Mere)	*Douglas Griffiths*	52
Hadlow Rd. Railway Station, Willaston	*Mary Hodgson*	53
Willaston Mill	*Geraldine Green*	54
Finding Ice	*John Berry*	55
The Miners of Wirral	*Muriel Cordon*	56
Neston Ladies Day, 1971	*Sylvia Hikins*	57

Time Out	Bettina Jones	59
Ness Gardens	Valerie M. Carr	60
Quaker Graves, Burton	Jean Stanbury	62
A Burton Manor Collage	Gladys Mary Coles and Workshop poets	63
Lines Written in Burton Churchyard	Joan Hartley	64
The Light at Inner Marsh	Peter Walton	65
from: River Views	Marjorie Dennison	65
The Sands of Dee	Charles Kingsley	66
The Recusant (Puddington Manor)	Sandra Kirby	68
Backwater (Shotwick)	Edward Lloyd	69
The Cistercian Abbey of Stanlow	unknown Monk	70
Ellesmere Port from the M53	Sue Martin	71
The Fly Boat	Alan Davis	72
The Old Yew at Eastham	R. J. Gilpin	74
from: At Eastham on the Mersey (1850s)	Richard Crompton	74
Eastham Locks	Philip Bastow	75
Dibbinsdale	John Reynolds	76
Poulton Hall (1939)	Roger Lancelyn Green	77
The Ghost of Poulton Hall	Heather Wilson	78
The Battle of Brunanburh, 937	Anon. (Old English)	79
Sea-Change at Bromborough	Gordon Thompson	80
Worship Ancient and Modern	Linda Bradley	81
Spital Crossroads	Laura Plested	82
Bebington Church	Egerton Leigh	83
Storeton	John Reynolds	83
Port Sunlight Village	Robin Thomas	84
The Village	Sheila Parry	85
The Lady Lever Art Gallery		
1. The Scapegoat	Gladys Mary Coles	86
2. The Kelpie	Edmund Cusick	87
Ceramics	Gina Riley	88
Rock Ferry Afternoon	Jean Lewis	89
In Rock Park	Mary Brett	90
Rock Park	Barbara Hope Allan	91
Tranmere Basement Blues	Douglas Griffiths	92
Polling Station	Douglas Griffiths	92
57600 (Prenton, 1947)	I. H. Hanson	93
Inside the Williamson Art Gallery	Edward Lloyd	94
For the Centenary of Wilfred Owen	Gladys Mary Coles	95
Birkenhead Priory in 1777	William Roscoe	96
Birkenhead Priory, 1819	Thomas Whitby	96
Birkenhead Priory	Jean Stanbury	97
The Children's Graveyard	Jean Stanbury	98
The Opening of Birkenhead Docks (Song) 1847	Anon.	99
Morpeth Dock, Birkenhead	Heather Wilson	101
People's Carriage	Malcolm Chisholm	102
The Last Launching	Anne Green	103
Epitaph to Cammell Laird	Sandra Kirby	104
Talking Newspaper	Peggy Poole	105
The New Shopping Mall	Jean Lewis	106
The Theatre Ghost (The Little Theatre)	Don McLean	106
The Black Chair of Birkenhead	Gladys Mary Coles	107
Birkonian Childhood	Doris Lamount	108

Birkenhead Park	John Reynolds	108
Hamilton Square Haiku	Alan Stanbury	109
Hamilton Square	Kathleen Dhenin	109
The Mersey Railway	Malcolm Chisholm	110
Returning to Hamilton Square Station	Miriam Bennett	111
Historic Warships	Hilary Tinsley	112
from: Ships	Gus Halligan	112
The Strong Salt Winds at Liverpool	John E. M. Sumner	113
Somersault	Mary Brett	113
After Forty Years	John Masefield	114
Mersey Ferries	Philip Bastow	116
North End Girls (1950s)	Anne Green	117
The Roundabout Church (St James)	Denise O'Shea	118
Bidston Windmill	Jean Stanbury	119
Bidston Hill, Bidston Moss	Graeme Kenna	120
Bulrushes (Bidston Moss)	Gill Cheseldine	121
The Rose Hedge (Fender Valley)	Gill Cheseldine	122
Wreckers and Smugglers	Anon.	122
Pointers to the Past	Fay Eagle	123
Childhood Memory of Seacombe to New Brighton	Antoinette Loftus	124
Over the Water	Hilary Tinsley	125
New Brighton, February	Alison Chisholm	126
New Brighton Foreshore in Winter	Robin Thomas	126
The Tower Grounds	Sheila Holt	127
The Wirral Show	Ceri Courtenay	127
New Brighton Milestones	Jan Curran	128
Atherton Street, New Brighton	Tom Alsop	130
The Red Noses	Bill Heap	132
Dodge City, New Brighton	Aileen La Tourette	133
New Brighton Ghosts	Albert Morgan	134
New Brighton Window	Aileen La Tourette	136
Derby Baths, New Brighton 1949	Margot Hoerty	137
Mockbeggar	Brian Mitchell	138
Staying at Leasowe	Alison Chisholm	139
Banking on Moreton Cross	Gordon Thompson	140
Overchurch	Gina Southern	141
Arrowe Park	Angela Keaton	142
The Greasby Pump	Amitav Ghosh	143
Romans in Irby	Ceri Courtenay	144
George Congreve, First Vicar of Frankby	Alan Gaunt	146
Stranger God	John Curry	147
Dove Point, Meols	Dora Kennedy	148
The Submerged Forest, Meols 1636	Richard James	148
from: Hoylake, 1794	Anna Seward	149
Our Grendel	Diana Hendry	150
Birthstone	John Curry	151
The Ghostly Promenade	Jacqui Baker	152
Out of Bounds	Jacqueline Bartlett	153
Force 8	Peggy Poole	154
Winter Wirral Twilight	Tracy Smith	155
To Winifred on Hilbre	Alan Gaunt	156
A Pleasant Place to Live	Elsie Williams	157
Index of Poets / Illustrators		158
Acknowledgements		160

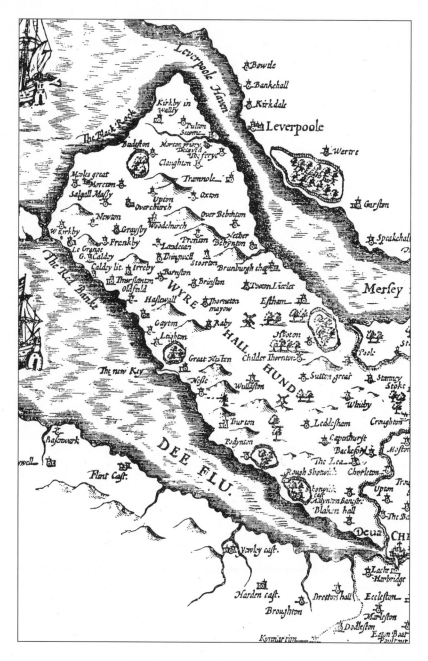

Map of Wirral from John Speed's
Map of Cheshire, 1611

THE HUNDRED OF WIRRAL
A 'found' poem devised from William Webb's description of the
Hundred of Wirral in *King's Vale Royal of England (1622)*

a long square
a rhomboid
its sides not straight lines
opposite ends not equal in their distance

the sole of a lady's left foot pantosole —
north-west end
encompassed by the sea,
narrowing both ways
between Bebington and Oldfield;
widens itself either way
to Stanney and Burton
where it is broadest

then narrowing again till it points
with the tip of the toe
upon Chester liberties

a languet of the land
promontory of the mainland
shooting into the sea
Dee-mouth
the Merzey

Gladys Mary Coles

Note: William Webb was Clerk to the Mayor's courts of Chester.
pantosole — lady's shoe
languet — little tongue

Wirral - Wirheal (mentioned in the Anglo-Saxon Chronicle). The
place name means 'myrtle-corner' (*wir* - myrtle; *heal* - corner);
the plant bog-myrtle once grew on the peninsula in profusion.

The Hundred - a division of land (Anglo-Saxon)

THE DEE

Before the Roman Legions came, I was.
Deva of Celtic tribesmen I, the Dee.
Locked in an ice age iron grip I lay
Waiting the kiss of sun to set me free.

Within my arm rose many a sheltering wall,
Norse, Saxon, Norman, all were one to me.
I took my toll and went upon my way,
My task to flow, my aim to reach the sea.

Deep lay my channel, golden were my sands,
Broad-mouthed I launched an army to the west.
King, freemen, pirates came to seek my aid
And patiently I bore them on my breast.

All have gone, another age has set
An enemy upon my shore, in greed,
And I who swept like sunlight to the deep
Flow sullen, lifeless, harnessed by a reed.

Dora Kennedy

THE MERSEY

I am the English sea-queen; I am she
Who made the English wealthy by the sea.

The street of this my city is the tide
Where the world's ships, that bring my glory, ride.

Far as the tide along my highway swings,
The iron of my shipwrights clangs and rings.

Far inland as the gulls go are my stores,
Where the world's wealth is lockt with iron doors.

And these my merchants gather day by day
The wealth I bring, the wealth I send away.

John Masefield
from *A Masque of Liverpool*

West Kirby
to
Gayton

From Blacon Point to Hillbree,
A squirrel may leap from tree to tree.

Anon. Old Rhyme

The Wirral Horn

The earliest mention of Wirral in poetry

from SIR GAWAIN AND THE GREEN KNIGHT

He had no friend but his horse in the forest and hills,
no man on his march to commune with but God,
till anon he drew near unto Northern Wales.
All the isles of Anglesey he held on his left,
and over the fords he fared by the flats near the sea,
and then over by the Holy Head to high land again
in the wilderness of Wirral: there wandered but few
who with good will regarded either God or mortal.
And ever he asked as he went on of all he met
if they had heard any news of a knight that was green
in any ground thereabouts, or of the Green Chapel.
And all denied it, saying nay, and that never in their lives
a single man had they seen that of such colour could be.

late 14th C.   *trans. J. R. Tolkien*

THE SHRINE OF ST. HILDEBURGH
ON HILBRE ISLAND

Dryshod o'er sands twice every day
The pilgrims to the shrine find way:
Twice every day the waves efface
Of staves and sandalled feet the trace.

Anon. Old Rhyme

FROM HILBRE ISLAND

Dissolution of day
on the estuary,
night's advance
on the evening tide;
and I, rock-lichen, cling
listening to sea-distance,
the murmur of a harmony
within a greater harmony

while from the fretted shore
humanity emits
a thousand brutish sounds
diffused and lost:

as on a distant plain
the sound of centuries repeats
and noise of conflict boils
from blue-skinned warriors
or scaly knights who swarm
like early amphibians
floundering, sea-emerged.

Gladys Mary Coles

MR BLUE

Flitting over
The wild, white wave crests
Of the estuary,
You came,
For all the world
Flying like a little tern.

Fluttering onto
The floating, island haven
Of our ship
To escape
The snapping-sharp
Beaks of gulls,
Skuas and shearwaters,
You enhanced our boyish dreams.

John Curry

WEATHER RHYME

He who looks along the Dee,
Be he wise, will surely see —
If the far-off's clear as glass,
Rain will shortly come to pass.
But if there's September haze,
He'll the next day surely praise.

Anon

WET SPRING BANK HOLIDAY, DEE ESTUARY

Most of the view you have to imagine
when grey presents its variations —
the opposite coast ghosting back.
Absent first are the field shapes,
a green collage of hills,
precise definition of copse and farm,
the massed browns of Holywell;
next, Moel-y-Parc retracts its long antenna.
Under a gauze of rain, the outlined hills —
curvilinear, cut-off, cauled —
disappear in the drowned distance.

From both the estuary's shores
this same shroud separating
coasts, cliffs, the sprinkling of estates
whose lights at night are fallen galaxies —
all dissolve in the vanishing trick.

The metallic Dee divides
yet magnetises shore to shore.
Staring across from each side, eyes
watch like wildlife in undergrowth;
or binocularised, strain to reduce the miles,
capture circles of someone else's space.
Dunlin, redshank, gull, in flight
link coast to coast invisibly,
alight on unseen sand-banks.

Always there's this yearning to connect —
the views are never sufficient,
yet every fade-out seems somehow a death.

Gladys Mary Coles

WHITSUN WEST KIRBY

(i)

the Whitsun tides are out:
paint peels from bare hulls strewn
over the mud-flats

a lark cries her protection above cliffs
where red soil still trickles down
after heavy spring storms

dogs splash in the retreating eddies
as the beach waits for children and spades
all the hours spent till now
making those yet to come seem
more precious still
somehow
salted with promise

(ii)

everyone's out in their cars and vans
hair flows through sun-roofs

shorts and sunglasses, snorkles and boards,
plastic bottles, tin cans and apple cores
strewn over the sands

while wanton bodies, pale as lurpak,
snake behind the dunes

here warmed skin smells different
and, tasted, bites the tongue

here shrieking laughter shards the air
as hidden passions find new ploys
rolling down over slides of sand
picnicing mouth to mouth

until the moon hangs out to signal dusk

car doors bang
the bubbling afternoon dissolves

everyone takes home a cup of sand
to ply memory with at night
when even the crispest sheets make do as dunes

Dymphna Callery

WEST KIRBY BEACH, NEW YEAR'S EVE

The sky and the sea
glittering,
whispering waves
rushing in;
wind whips the skin
from your cheekbones,
salt stings your cold lips.

The dog fidgets, forages,
snuffling and shuffling
in the sand,
his lead tugging,
cutting your fingers
thrust
deep into your pockets.

Far away,
fireworks fizzing,
the festivities beyond the shore
celebrating the new decade,
a million
and a million miles away.

I was there, didn't you see me?
I was always there.

Carole Baldock

TELL'S TOWER

Tell: Champion Rough Coat of England.
Painted by Landseer in 1869. Died 1871.

For years it stood alone
in the grounds of Hilbre House
that became the Speaker's home;
a monument to guide travellers
across miles of estuary
like the lighthouse at Talacre
on the opposing Celtic coast.

Erected over the grave
of a champion St. Bernard
"noble and of undaunted courage"
the circular tower is now
part of a modern bungalow,
titillated with ruched curtains
and ripe pear carpets, struggling
to retain significance.

One April I had to call on Selwyn Lloyd
to apologise for a missed appointment
telling lies about being unwell
not wanting to admit slothful habits.
Standing among primroses and bluebells
in the tower's shelter he confided,
while picking me spring flowers,
his intention, on return to London,
to rule the phrase "a pack of lies"
as unparliamentary, which in future
would be disallowed in the House of Commons.
Was he saying he saw through my excuses?

Rain and wind test the turret's
sandstone that rises from red brick;
today, walking my dog on the shore,
I contemplate courage and truth.

Peggy Poole

ON HILBRE

Here the wind is stiff as a brush,
creaming the waves on the sand,
scuffing up seal songs and shore birds
like dust thrown about in eddies.

On the dry, myriad-year walls
there is a red scurf: the brush
eats into stone and spins it out
leaving eye-sockets and bone flowers.

Heather and thrift have grown hard,
stems smoky with cliff-top incense,
whose domain lies from here to Anglesey,
to Ireland and Cornwall and beyond.

Always the same watery voices
and the clean wild scrubbing of wind,
and the soil glinting with sand, pared down
and the tight black mats of plants.

St. Mary in Lleyn and Our Lady of Hilbre
and St. Tudno at Orme, all bounded
by this dry wind and its carved stone:
its otherworldly poverty of place

splendid with flowers, lavender and pink.
We have nowhere to go but within,
nothing to remember but the old, beating wind
and everything clean to taste and wonder at.

Sue Craggs

TAKERS
The Cockle War, Dee Estuary

The tide pulls back, exposes the beds
of cockles, vulnerable in glossy mud.
Motorbikes advance, reverberate
like low-flying planes.
We hear these daily manoeuvres
of the cockle convoy; from the cliff
we see them out there, black gulls
scavenging. They fill the gullets
of sacks, packing carts their tractors tug.

Days, months,
mining the mud
they're strung-out pegs on a line.
Marauding, guarding their ground,
they ward off incomers, compete
for the cockle coinage,
those shells of lime with age-revealing rings:
two years, one, none —
too small to take, yet taken.

Calling, one to another, they forage
in families, sons snared in their fathers' trade.
While nearby, on a sea-walled lake,
the leisure lads in shiny wet-suits race
clinging to their stained-glass sails.

Today, a gritty wind,
the boat-yard chinking,
all verticals an instrument.
Still the cocklers smudge the horizon —
dark question marks. Their voices
flung, buffeted like kites.

Here on the shore
the tide's tossed jokes. We find
a bloated hand (sludge-filled glove),
drowned pale hair (meshed sack-string),
swollen bladders (sliced-bread bags),
split leggings splayed across the rocks.

This detritus reminds us of ourselves —
users and spenders all our days.
We collect the spent shells. Sand,
home to other creatures, falls
through our fingers.

Gladys Mary Coles

TRAIN BOYS

At ten to nine at Kirby Park
   the train came steaming in,
To disembark the Calday boys ·
   with rowdy youthful din.
To scramble over Caldy Hill
   was daily their intent,
With boisterous noise up wooden steps
   began the long ascent.
The sandstone cottages they passed,
   then by the 'Ring o'Bells',
Through Wetstone Lane they reached the hill
   where larks' sweet singing swells.

They reached the ridge where views extend
   across the Irish Sea,
To Lakeland Hills and Blackpool Tower,
   the Ormes and Anglesey.
Below the hill the ancient school's
   red sandstone buildings drew
The boys into its warm embrace
   to kindle minds anew.

At ten past four the bells rang out,
   the daily learning done,
The satchels packed with homework tasks,
   they set off on their run.
Where once again they bounded down
   the runnels on the hill,
No time to look to Hilbre Isle
   nor hear the birds' sweet trill.
The engine's whistle echoed out
   along the banks of Dee,
Just time to snatch some buns and batch
   from Riley's bakery.
A friendly call would ring out loud
   to urge the thin blue line

To hasten to the train's good crew
   who daily kept on time.
They've long long gone this group so strong
   in cameraderie,
The train-boys' song and laughter long
   are just a memory.

Philip Bastow

The Wirral Way - the scenic West Kirby to Hooton railway line, closed in 1962, became the 12 mile footpath officially opened in 1973 as Wirral Country Park, the first Country Park in Britain. The Visitor Centre is at Thurstaston.

A CHILD'S PATH (The Wirral Way)

They say that once the trains went by.
Now it's a path and trees and sky.
At Cuckoo Lane all's white with may,
the hawthorn on the Wirral Way.

When apple blossom filled the air
and lightly fell upon my hair—
it seems so long ago, that day,
while walking on the Wirral Way.

That day I thought, "How long ago
the cherry flowered soft as snow."
I think I like bird cherry best,
with all its boughs in whiteness dressed.

Each day's so long, and yet l've spent
a host since cherry came and went.
I thought that it would stand and stay
forever on the Wirral Way.

But now it's hawthorn, washed with rain;
will cherry never come again?
For next will be, I heard them say,
wild roses on my flowering Way.

Bruce Withers

THANK YOU, MR STAPLEDON

Thank you Mr Stapledon for walks I've so enjoyed
The broken tracks of silver birch away from city noise
The woodland beauty holding one entranced within its hand
The squirrels, rabbits, moles and voles in magic Olaf's land.

My home sits humbly by your woods, my windows blessed with
                                                              views
My life affected by your gift, my soul in debt to you.
Your name is now forever blessed in many Wirral hearts
Such gift, such magnaminity, your woods set you apart.

J. M. Corfe

Note: *Olaf Stapledon (1886-1950), a philosopher and Science
Fiction writer who lived most of his life at Caldy.*

A WINDOW ON THE WIRRAL

Winter mornings,
when the sun springs into your eyes,
and the sky looks upside-down
pastel clouds fan out above
a wide stretched swathe of blue,
punctuated by sparkling flocks of wheeling birds -
glittering princes emerging from a spell?
We waken sometimes on days like this,
from winter's dark enchantment.

Winter evenings,
when the world is almost dusk,
just the red roofs flare and glow,
and the tips of stark tree branches
are brushed with transient tints.
Dark descends, leaving in the West
one last lingering streak of light ...
God's left a lamp on for us,
shining under Heaven's front door.

Carole Baldock

CALDY

If your soul is seeking solace and you have a yen to stray,
Just steal away to Caldy and foot it all the day.
Begin at Barton's Cross by the chapel on the turn,
Decipher the epistle carved upon the stone.
Thus enriched by simple words, erected on Ascension Day
Almost a century ago, now wander on your way.

Pass the cottaged hamlet and the manor stately, grand,
Bear by a bridle cutting, horseshoes in the sand.
Inching up the leafy passage, cloaked by bruised and lichened
walls
Ivy gripping, ivy dripping, wren flitting, coal-crow calls.
Stop a moment just to listen; a tom-tit plays his perky pipe
And the piping answer echoes from his not too distant wife.

Dropping deeper in a hollow, mossy briar banks creep knee high
The first primrose poses pretty for the dappled winter sky.
Take the road past peeping villas, wattle winding to a wood
Sloping softly to a field edge, squirrels scatter in the mud;
Gazing right, a pointing steeple where the roaring road carves through;
Ahead, a moved mansion, Cheshire chimneys climb to view.

When your eyes have feasted fully on verdant Frankby Hill,
And the spirit's soaked the sweetness of solitude tranquil,
Curl along a kerneled carpet of chestnut, pine and oak,
Broad beech stretching limbs to Heaven eye you as you walk.
Glide gently through a ballroom of birch beauties silver-dressed,
The shy jay flies furtive through their mantles, purple laced.

Cross the lane at dormied dwelling where Snow White might have
stayed,
Rugged rhododendrons, ragged roots the path has paved;
Just a few feet further, a clearing broadly bright
Opens up a picture that will make the senses light.
Beyond, the sparkling Dee wraps the slumbering hills of Wales.

Lonely isle of holy Hilbre where St. Hildeburgh knelt in prayers
And heather spreads her blanket, gilded golden with furze flowers.
Rest on the bench for Norma Claire, marvel at God's powers.
Rest and be thankful, traveller, then choose your homeward way
But steal again to Caldy when you have a yen to stray.

Mary White

LINES FROM MALTA, 1917

There's bright sunshine here in Malta, while at home are fog and rain,
With the wet wind on the uplands and the floods down in the plain.
But in spite of winter's weather I would far, far rather be
In the wide, sweet, open country 'twixt the Mersey and the Dee.

Though the woods are bare and leafless and the song-birds all are fled
Though the flowers in the gardens and the hedgerows all are dead;
And the wet west wind comes sweeping in across the Irish Sea,
To wake the foam on Mersey Bar and flood the Sands o' Dee;

Yet, spite of wintry storm or rain or fog, I love it all,
And long to be on Thurstaston as evening shadows fall;
For no sight is half so beautiful or half so dear to me,
As the stormy, golden sunset o'er the gleaming Sands o' Dee.

And when the war is over, with what joy shall I return,
To the fields and paths and commons and the woods for which I
yearn,
To the moors and the uplands, and the salt kiss of the sea,
In the Hundred of the Wirral 'twixt the Mersey and the Dee.

Frank Jocelyn Priest

HAIKU

Weather-worn wall, glints
showing glazed secrets of sand
turning slow to stone.

Linda Bradley

THE WIRRAL WAY

Declared redundant, the branch-line closed,
but those who laid its track across the Wirral
are still remembered here with gratitude,
for rails have been dismantled to provide
a way for ramblers. Safe from busy roads
it runs through fields with hedges on each side
grass underfoot. Wild flowers grow on the banks,
birds haunt the hedgerows, while beyond
cows graze the meadow-grass scarce lifting heads
to watch the folk on foot; no more disturbed by
clatter of carriages, chatter of steel on steel,
hissing of steam or high-pitched warning whistle
they munch in peace.
          Some way further along
the track enters a sandstone cutting, losing
its sense of space. Here it seems narrower, darker,
deprived of sun, the redness of the walls
obscured erratically by lichens, ferns
or damp green slime; in other places
scored by indelible grooves made by machines
which gouged the cut. Underfoot is often muddy;
weird hump of moss and matted growth
is a mysterious menace. The place smells rank.
Nobody lingers here.
          Much further on again
is space to linger. The soil turns sandy,
whin bushes and sharp blackthorn grow
and air comes tanged from the Dee —
odd silted estuary of marsh and mud,
catching the light, reflecting sky, or
stretching its gleam of waters at high tide
across to the hills of Wales. These sudden views
are glimpsed through hedges, between trees.
The curlews call, the dainty oyster-catchers
place long red legs with care among the stones,
while time itself hangs poised and motionless
on hovering sea-gull's wings — a therapy
amid twentieth-century bustle, for still small voice
will never be redundant.

Mary Hodgson

from: A JANUARY WALK

Hoar frost;
white mist covers the river,
the hillsides washed in weak morning sun.

Threading back-alleys by stone cottages,
down between brambles and bracken
we clamber cautiously over
rocky outcrops slippery with ice.

A brief rest in the Dale
to peel off gloves and woollies,
search bare branches
for that blackbird lustily singing,
the sun warming upturned faces.

Breathless from toiling up the other side,
we lean on a farm fence,
watch steaming, shaggy calves
feed in the open-sided barn.
Dung rich on the frosty air.

Mary Brett

HILLBARK

A leafy green forbidden way
lured me to the house that day,
Strictly Private the sign read:
Temptation teased, I crept ahead,
Bearing round a silent path,
The risk was worth a watchman's wrath.
I never will forget the sight
A splendid mansion black and white
Dazzling patterned plaster daubed
Chevron crossed circled clubbed
Chimneys coiled like barley sticks
Sandstone slabs and rustic bricks,
A wondrous scene to gaze upon
Yet it looked lonely and forlorn.

No smoke curled from a towering stack
No scolding voice to drive me back;
A timbered porch, a cobbled yard
Grass steps leading to a sward.
One wing rose three latticed floors
Frilled gables carved, thick panelled doors.
An old ha-ha sloped to the west
To pleasure grounds where magpies nest
In scented pines. Meadows opened wide —
There squirrels ply and foxes hide
And birches plumed in purple lace,
Where people walk in leisured pace.

From window panes no eyes did peer
To wonder why I trespassed near,
But eerie feelings came to me
I felt the house was watching me.
Without malignity it seemed to say
Am I being left to face decay.
Proud edifice of Bidston Hill
Moved to this site the more tranquil.
A fit home for a wealthy peer
I'm just over my hundreth year.
When hard times came I was sold
To be a haven for the old.

Now they've moved too, that's my sad tale
And once again I'm up for sale.
No buyers come. Oh, what's my fate,
I'll cost so much to renovate.
Just think — a prince once so loved me
He built my twin in Germany.
But now, I'm empty and alone
And that's why I look so forlorn.

If thought between a house and man
Can be exchanged, then I for one
Will say for you a solemn prayer
That one will come who'll really care
And love you as a work of art
And cherish you with all his heart.

Mary White

THÓR'S STONE

Sandstone rock, red-rock sand,
Undulating, bouldering,
Sight to remember.

Underfoot soft,
Sometimes crunchy,
Sandstone pulverised, grainy.

Thór's stone beckons,
Spirits and legends,
Surrounded by red-glow aura.

Desert-sand, desert-stones,
Lingering there
Through the ages.

Men of war, helmets shining
Left their boats.
Thor's stone beckons, spirits dancing.

Northern Lights,
Twinkling stars
Memories from yonder.

God of Thunder, men of war
Unite, sacrificial,
In red-glow aura.

Norma Jamieson

Note: *The Viking Norse settled extensively in Wirral, a colony with its own administration throughout the tenth and eleventh centuries. Their first leader was Ingimund. Place names such as Meols, Tranmere, Raby and Thingwall are evidence of Norse settlement; the huge red-sandstone block, Thór's Stone at Thurstaston Hill, is named after the Norse god.*

WIRRAL COUNTRY PARK CENTRE, THURSTASTON

Set amongst the leafy green, barely seen
the educational timber hut
peeps like a nest –
for the children, ramblers and country-keen,
the wildlife lovers who linger
and traipsing tourists who rest.

The long cliff-top stretching
yields to daytime human flocks
passing by ponds, bramble and sandstone walls.

Wildlife and screeching on the green.
Later, black clouds and fading light,
and a lonely monument
where people have been.

The Wirral Way
takes the people away –
wild-flower fresh,
unfolding foaming foliage.
Cyclists and back-packers race,
their milestones each sandstone bridge.

Long strands of estuary shimmer
as dark now unfolds.
The first fox soon fumbles
from the undergrowth, foraging
for scraps left by the daytime droves.
In the all-black night
sky and cliff blend.
The Centre is closed.

Lindsay Coles

MANCUNIANS IN THE DALES
(With apologies to William Allingham's Fairies)

Up the heathery mountain,
down the slippery trails,
four boys and Grandad
exploring Heswall Dales.

Wellie boots and trainers
go with hop and skip,
anoraks and bobble hats
and Man United strip.

Standing on the highest peak,
mountaineers take stock
of rooftops and treetops
and cliffs of reddest rock.

Another land beyond the sea
that Grandad says is Wales,
but we know it's America
we see from Heswall Dales.

Deep in the valley
trees are good to climb,
we'd reach the highest branches
if only we had time.

See where something's dug a den
hidden by the rocks,
maybe it's a savage wolf
but Grandad says a fox.

Time for going home now,
creeping slow as snails,
anoraks and bobble hats
leaving Heswall Dales.

Freda Rankin

AT THE HIGHEST POINT: POLL HILL

A rotund, concrete water tower squats
outside the fence, poised on the garden's edge
where common land encroaches, seeps over lawns
pinned down with rosebeds and floral borders.

Beyond the perimeters, silver birch,
a stumbling crowd of them,
threading surface roots, broken branches;
a litter of growth, maturity, passing on.

Over stone walls, a donkey's raw throat
once fractured the air like a creaking gate,
rusty like the red of the sandstone cutting
that slices the outcrop beyond.

This forlorn creature, tangle of wire wool,
wore skin like sackcloth and disappointment:
the dome of his hilltop home, all sky,
blue grey, white; the rattling winds of it.

Miriam Bennett

HESWALL BEACONS

Beyond the frenzied tumult of the trees
that jostle in a wild exotic dance,
I glimpse the fretfulness of rain-soaked seas.
This wilderness alive - it was by chance
I chose today to walk across its past,
where once a private garden bloomed and thrived.
What would old ghosts make of these stark contrasts,
should they return to see how much survived?

And yet it holds a beauty all its own,
and soothing on this stormiest of days,
ten secret acres where the foxes roam
and weasels steal through ancient tangleways.

Perhaps the Beacons' spirits, after all,
might yet approve if they should be recalled.

Kit Jackson

from: **THE PIRATE OF PARK WEST**

Down there, where Flintshire's mountains
    Form a background to the sea,
When the sun's descending fountains
    Burnish up the sands of Dee;
Far from mankind's garish glamour
    And the Gold God's chuckling glee,
Far from the city's noise and clamour,
    With the children, I would be.

Fred Bower
(The Stonemason Poet of Heswall)

SUNSET OVER THE DEE

Over the Dee, above North Wales
Strange clouds form like the hand of doom:
Spread tentacles, arms, cloaks and veils
In amber, ochre, grey, maroon,
Clawing their way across the skies,
Creeping towards us as we stand.
Each shaft of sparkling sunlight dies
And leaves behind an ochre land.
But look! Beyond the purpled hill
Clear skies of silver, gold and blues
Increase in glory until they fill
The space above; then hope renews.
The umbrous clouds have onward rolled,
Their deep, dark tones turned red and gold.

Patricia Minter

HESWALL DAYS

I built dams
water-courses,
lakes and runs,
with sticks for a shovel
and hands for cranes.

I formed the mud,
placed the stones,
decided the path
the water would take.

Summer on the beach,
winter on the dales,
with running stream
and stagnant pond.

I built dams.

Martin Bennett

LOWER VILLAGE, HESWALL

A necklace of shops
jewels this small village
and sparkles for our attention
alive in the morning sunlight.

Approaching by car,
forced to slow down,
we weave our way around the narrow road.

All manner of life is served here
for those who have not yet
felt the supermarket lure.

For them a remembered name
and kindly smile more important
than the production line tills.

A veil of opulence clothes these shops.

Unchanged over generations
everything provided in one timeless zone.

Jane Brassey

REMEMBRANCE DAY
HESWALL LOWER VILLAGE

Like blind ghosts the clouds came
bumbling and stumbling
piling grey on grey
down Moel Famau -
across Flint and Halkyn -
onward over the silver snaking Dee

until a thin drizzle fell
like a veil -
a 'drawing down of blinds'
obscuring, obliterating,
closing down the estuary.

Then, on fretful gusts
came the shuttered sound
of St. Peter's bells
carrying brokenly
the half-muffled round
of the Grand Sire.

One by one they ceased -
until only the tenor remained
its last notes tolling sad
on the rain-soaked village.

It was eleven o'clock.

Time to remember

Jacqui Baker

Note: *'a drawing down of blinds' from 'Anthem for Doomed Youth' by Wilfred Owen (1893-1918).*

THE DEE SHORE AT HESWALL

Old houses grey with wind and sun so placed
Along the airy margin of the Dee,
That each in turn looks out across the waste
Of drifting sand and shallow to the sea:

Old boats low-moored upon the channel's edge,
Asleep and dreaming of tomorrow's tide;
A mist of nets along the paling-ledge,
A spread of sail-cloth that the sun has dried:

A group of fisherfolk with southern eyes,
And accents borrowed from a bygone day,
The scream of seagulls and the far-off cries
Of wild-fowl flying home from Hilbre way:

This is Old Haven and the place I love;
I love the sea-wall that its tides have broke,
The sandy shallows and the gulls above,
The houses, boats and nets and fisherfolk.

John Pride
(c. 1930)

from: **GAYTON WAKE, 1804**

Up rose the sun, the sky was clear,
And gently ebbed the Dee;
The winds of heaven were fast asleep,
Though Gayton all was glee.

The lads of Wirral came in crowds,
The nymphlets neat and trim,
To stay at home on such a day
Is very near a sin.

And Love, who never missed a Wake,
Brought quivers filled with darts;
He'd much to do on all such days,
And wounds a world of hearts.

And Cambria's youth from Edwin's shores,
An annual voyage take,
What lass would stay on that side of Dee,
When Love's at Gayton Wake?

Youth, manhood, age, even childhood came,
To share this jocund day;
The hedges shone with gaudy shops,
And Gayton all was gay.

From Hoylake Hall to Gayton came
Fine ladies, gentlemen;
They come, my friends to look at *you*
And *you* may look at them.

The day wax'd short — the Wake grew thin,
Some sail'd adown the Dee.
Whilst others tugg'd against the tide,
And rowed to Hilburee.

Richard Llwyd

*Gayton
to
Burton*

from: **LYCIDAS**

Where were ye nymphs when the remorseless deep
Closed o'er the head of your loved Lycidas?
For neither were ye playing on the steep,
Where your old Bards, the famous Druids lie,
Nor on the shaggy top of Mona high,
Nor yet where Deva spreads her wizard stream:
Ay me, I fondly dream!
Had ye been there — for what could that have done?
What could the Muse herself that Orpheus bore,
The Muse herself, for her inchanting son
Whom universal nature did lament,
When by the rout that made the hideous roar,
His gory visage down the stream was sent,
Down the swift Hebrus to the Lesbian shore...

Ay me! Whilst thee the shores, and sounding seas
Wash far away, where e'er thy bones are hurled,
Whether beyond the stormy Hebrides,
Where thou perhaps under the whelming tide
Visit'st the bottom of the monstrous world;
Or whether thou to our moist vows denied,
Sleep'st by the fable of Bellerus old,
Where the great vision of the guarded mount
Looks toward Namancos and Bayona's hold;
Look homeward angel now, and melt with ruth.
And, o ye dolphins, waft the hapless youth...

Thus sang the uncouth Swain to the oaks and rills,
While the still morn went out with sandals gray;
He touched the tender stops of various quills,
With eager thought warbling his Doric lay:
And now the sun had stretched out all the hills,
And now was dropt into the western bay;
At last he rose, and twitched his mantle blue:
Tomorrow to fresh woods and pastures new.

John Milton

Note: *Milton was deeply moved by the death of Edward King, a brilliant scholar, drowned on 10 August, 1637, off the Welsh coast when his ship was wrecked in passage from Chester to Ireland. King was the son of Sir John King, Secretary of State for Ireland.*

SPRING TIDE IN THE DEE ESTUARY

This is an occasion: today
the tide is due at Parkgate.
Once an everyday affair
with ships sailing to Dublin,
now a phenomenon, conjured up
by strong winds and a spring tide.
We say, "All on one side like Parkgate"
and so it is; massed dwellings,
its famous school on this side,
on the other wild marshes stretch
towards the slopes of Wales.

Spectators line what used to be the quay,
(inclement weather, records say,
prevented Handel from embarking here
with his Messiah). Pools form
and a skim of water covers grass and sedge.
Over the sea-wall, children, armed
with sticks, attempt to rescue mice
marooned on flotsam,
catcall after a solitary rat, slinking
half-immersed in scum.
Pose for photographs —
with sandbanks submerged, birds
stream in to the sanctuary.

Water deepens but the influx is brief;
unobtrusively the tide recedes,
visitors resume their promenade,
old cottages laze in the sun.
Among the cobbles *Nelson* is spelt out
in black round stones.
Is it a tribute to the great man,
dallying maybe with his Emma,
the blacksmith's daughter from Ness
just up the road?

A local lad enlightens us —
a child, a boy, was lost like Kingsley's

Mary, who went to call the cattle home
across these hidden sands.

As tides go it is a poor show
but we are satisfied,
today we saw the tide in at Parkgate.

Dora Kennedy

EMMA LYON

I met her in her father's forge where I had led the mare,
And gladly would I cast a shoe to see a face so fair.
I walked the long Parade when pretty nurses met the tide,
I loitered by the Neston Cross but none like her espied.
I loosed a spring to find her but the blacksmith shook his head
"The lass is down in London town with gentlefolk," he said.
I mounted with a heavy heart and little did I guess
That I would see that lovely face two hundred miles from Ness.
But yesterday she passed me in the royal park at Hyde,
Quite early in the morning when the lords and ladies ride.
Had I but seen the chance of it as I had well the mind,
I should have seized a livery-hack and followed up behind.
"Why there's my pretty Cheshire maid," I said to one beside:
"O, no sir, you mistake. That's Lady Hamilton," he cried.

John Pride (c.1930)

Note: *Amy Lyon. later Emma Lady Hamilton and mistress of Lord Nelson, was born at Ness, 26th April, 1765. She returned on a visit to Parkgate during summer, 1784.*

ASHFIELD HALL FARM

A pheasant strides for cover
over dead grass, heads broken,
into stripped brambles
summer's bounty eaten or withered.

Hidden hare leaps and sprints away
dog chasing through the sodden fields
until, tongue lolling, he returns and sniffs
the empty tussock, hope denied.

Solitary the heron stands
on one leg waiting, waiting, still
as the air he breathes, scented with fox,
and startled mallards leave the secret water.

Arrowed geese honk their flight
over this farmland, husbanded into life
by those whose love and expertise
fashioned our countryside, dying now.

The golf course waits; walk in peril
risking the pot shot warning you
from ancient ways diverted or ignored;
there will be no hedges here.

Lorna Home

Note: *Ashfield Hall lies behind Parkgate. Built in 1818 it was demolished after the Second World War. Aerial photographs show evidence of crop markings similar to those on Roman sites. Before the Norman Conquest Neston was linked to the Church of Secular Canons. Parkgate's name derives from Neston Park enclosed as a deer park in 1250 for 350 years.*

TO A SCULPTURED HEAD

What are you doing, Oh Cheshire Cat,
in the chapel at Brimstage Hall,
when you should be over at Daresbury
with the Queen and Alice and all?

It's been said that your head is a lion's,
the crest of a Brimstage knight,
without a paw and never a tail,
how can we tell which is right?

Maybe your grin does look like a snarl
and is there a trace of a mane?
Yet when I look, in my ALICE book,
you are there! Exactly the same.

Dora Kennedy

ALMOND TREES AT CLATTERBRIDGE, 1995

The ward overlooks the back of Pathology
red-brick and functional, unadorned, stark,
grey concrete paving and green-painted handrails,
spaces for cars of consultants to park.

Grass covers sparsely the scars of development,
nothing for butterflies, nothing for bees,
but corporate grouping of NHS conifers
shelters and succours young almond trees.

Delicate glow in the sunshine of morning,
blossoms that dance on branches that sway,
rose-coloured heralds of springtime's late coming
lighten and brighten a hospital day.

March winds may toss them in cruel commotion,
petals are scattered till clouds have passed over,
and sunset's reflection will light them again.

Freda Rankin

MID-WIRRAL LANES, AUTUMN RIDE

Through Thornton Hough, Willaston and Raby –
the wind picks up
lifting the leaves in copper coppices.
Clouds move like smoke smudging
heathery lilac over Halkyn,
deepening to bilberry the Welsh mountains.

Rising over Willaston the tall mill
and poplars in a sunset glow
are a Dutch winter painting.
The last flickers of sun flame over our faces,
cold flares resting red on Raby's road.

Passing the dark mere, up by Poulton's Hall –
old oaks creaking; branches
crashing with squirrels;
estate fields soaking in the final glow.

Farmhouse lights are on,
their warmth waxing before
curtains are pulled, and the sky
purples over into dusk.

Ceri Courtenay

THORNTON HOUGH

A pastoral dream of Victorian men
who had visions of lasting monuments
to their lives and times.
This village remains their testimony.
The Gothic styles of Joseph Hirst,
the shop and cottages, church and school.
The extra clock face just for him to see.

No more dank cottages of thatch and wattle,
but solid stone from nearby quarries.

Then came Lever, growing fast.
His cottages in black and white,
in Folds along the village green.
He also built a church — in Norman style,
a bigger school, a village club.
A smithy with a chestnut tree
and farms all round, in country air.

The village stands the test of time,
a green oasis to pass through in your car.

Betty Hodges

SCARECROW FESTIVAL, Thornton Hough

Instead of scaring they unify people:
families walk from Raby and Clatterbridge
all brought together by simplicity
like flames drawn through the straw of a wicker man.

They're propped like Guy Fawkes effigies
from Humpty Dumpty to Harry Potter's ring.
Theme upon theme in woven straw: even Laurel and Hardy
connive in the carnival. Some stroll by, alive,
complete with acoustics; others, top-hatted
turn a rotary wheel: face-painted humans
bring effigies to life, caught up in the competition.

Jubilee queens sit amongst the generations
watch ferret-racing and dog-pulled pails on carts.
A floppy hat complete with resting crow
leaps out at you unawares; scarecrows
hang from mock-tudor doorways and beams
like rural harvest fertility mascots.

Some are staked in pretty flowerbeds
not scaring a single bee; keeping a happy vigil
over charity stalls, classic cars, clay shooting,
bouncy drome and fairground stuffed with pleasure.
Thornton Hough echoes from the thatched pavilion.

Ceri Courtenay

ALMOST AN ENCOUNTER (RABY MERE)

Who were they?
That couple,
That man and woman
Passed on a country road
One afternoon in winter.

They were still young
As far as could be seen,
But dressed in the style
Of a generation gone.

They walked hand in hand
Away from the lake.
A beauty spot in summer;
But now a grey disc, bleak,
Ringed with bare willows,
Like an eye expressing
Infinite sorrows.

And a snatch of speech
Heard as they passed
 Did little to solve the mystery,
'Say you love me, me, love me.'
It was not clear even if this
Was spoken in triumph or despair.

So they walked the straight, mist-shrouded road
Towards a village two miles away at least,
And night coming on.

Douglas Griffiths

HADLOW ROAD RAILWAY STATION, WILLASTON

The booking-office hall has luggage stacked;
time-tables show the times of local trains;
behind the glass-partition tickets are filed
ready for use, papers and ledgers lie
open for further entries; fire in the grate,
half-empty milk-bottle and porter's cap
all signify that life continues, yet
almost a quarter of a century has passed
since the branch line closed.

This is a superannuated railway station
restored as folk museum, the buildings painted,
clean and cared-for though trains have gone.
No railway lines extend beyond platform's end.
There are no passengers or staff. All here is quiet,
a Sleeping Princess world of sun and silence.

Such silence sets past echoes flying.
In booking-hall like this we bought our tickets
for childhood sea-side days; porters trundled
just such a trolley stacked with crates,
mail-sacks and holiday paraphernalia;
identical signs gave notice not to cross
rails when the train was signalled. In this quiet
now, I hear the distant rumble, growing thunder,
of the approaching monster, can feel the thrill
with which we stood on toes to catch first glimpse;
can see the rush-and-whoosh of its arrival, smell
the coal-fumes, hear shriek of expelled steam
as brakes come on, bravura of sparks and flame.

And in this noisy quiet that sense of childhood
timelessness returns. Those days seemed endless;
the journey on the train passing through fields
where rabbits scuttered was a lifetime;
the day upon the beach was an eternity
of sun and air.

     Solitary here
perched on this porter's trolley, I realise
it's not the relentless ticking-away of time
that we resent, in this world of non-stop movement,
but the passing of that time when time stood still.
It stands still here, and we can feel at rest.

Mary Hodgson

WILLASTON MILL

Shrouded, now, by time,
dust-covered and silent;
flour-shadowed ghosts
crowd round.

Where once was bustle
and laughter
as horse and man
pulled together
down the grain-laden lanes
to the Mill,
silence breathes.

Mighty arms stunted,
redundant, no longer wave.

Geraldine Green

FINDING ICE

Damp air,
Zested with the edge of morning's frost
Retreated before the sun's advent
As walkers gathered at Hinderton.

Last week, paths of mud
Had clutched with disgusting sound at boots,
Now rejected by cobbles of frozen hoof prints
Which hurt the feet and said
'You can't come in.'

Through the village path,
Vying for space with the spreading breath of warm dogs
They reached the estuary bank before the Harp.
Flasks vaporised, fragrant on the morning air
As sun turned fronds of tall grass
Taller than the walkers
Into flaming spears.
High up to the left Neston,
All sandstone and blue sky,
Below which,
Chunky horses in chunkier jackets
Stared with curious stupidity
At people choosing to walk
In the old rail cutting
Where pendant ice formed a crystal palace.
Icicles are rare now we're globally warmed.

Bubble, Squeak and Bangers,
Warm fire and good company
Ale aplenty to ease and massage
The day's aches
And lubricate the knees.

John Berry

THE MINERS OF WIRRAL

Early morning mists drift lazily
Over wide expanses of reed and sparkling water.
A peregrine glides watchfully
Quivering flocks of teal take flight.

Walkers tramp the shore path eagerly
Often unaware of the history at their feet.
Unnoticed, the sandstone blocks of the mine quay
And grassy hillocks of slag now softened by time.

Haunting reminders of centuries of human endeavour
When far out under the river bed
Men and boys struggled in waterlogged galleries
To recover coal and ensure their families were fed.

Labouring in shallow tunnels,
Where cut-through fossilised trees
Could drop from the roof like pillars of stone.
Just one of numerous dangers now unknown.

Small scars on the landscape, some faded photographs,
All that remain of a way of life.
Unknowing guardians in their safe haven
Of protected beauty, to-day the wildfowl flourish free from strife.

Muriel Cordon

Note: *Mining took place in the Neston area from around 1750 or even earlier. There were several smallish pits but Neston Colliery was the largest and the biggest employer in the area when it finally closed in 1927 (leaving around 150 people unemployed). Conditions were very difficult with galleries running out in places almost two miles under the river.*

NESTON LADIES DAY, 1971

Once-yearly rustic remnant
assembled memories among not so high-street throng,
Neston Ladies Day.
Civil servants tried to stop it carrying on.
Reason: economic computation, fiscal ruination,
treason, shouted Bridie, Nell and Rosemary.

So here's their day of days,
every bit of eighty in the shade,
perfect pictures, they stroll serenely,
forging the truth of their gentility.

The comings and goings of the past few hours,
will my feathers go with straw and flowers,
shall I leave the flags at yours or ours?
Having heard it all before,
their husbands sigh unlikely metaphors,
and, *what the hell, last year's will do*
becomes *tradition, perfectly divine;*
like diplomats, whose audience is due,
they leave their morals pegged out on the line.

These Neston Ladies make the sunbeams toil,
on crooks and staves,
dew-rousing shepherdesses
gather flocks and hollyhocks, face
still warm paths of righteousness
with half a yard of crinoline and lovelace,
Victorian flower power,
genuine outsize hippies.

To herald progress, a band, grey and maroon
with burnished brass blown slightly out of tune,
and high in air,
sustained by resolute hands,
the cloth of gold, annually unfurled,
here stands The Neston Female Friendly Society,
founded 1914,
(one man hot in his breeches
was heard to whisper, *witches*)
clasped like loves already loved,

now dare disturb our day with formulated phrase,
Bare Ye One Another's Burdens.

Under the flickering flags of Neston Cross
skip in the summer breezes at the door,
garlanded girls awaiting their tomorrow,
(the men in breeches, humbled, merely follow)
and ours,
already half gone,
find the lost days singing, singing along,
and gather mouthing, at summer's end, like swallows.

Here comes the mayor
walking motionless, erect,
gold chain, bowler hat,
his solemn gaze a monument
to the eternal intellect;
the teacher, mortar board ablaze,
his pupils fazed by his key stage,
walk as choir boys to the clergy,
piping slowly
another fading churchman at his song;
they came for fun,
white ruffed warblers with spuds behind their ears,
eyes gazing with the stars, and spears.
Singing masters, holy fire, civic throng,
all that cacophony of sound passes by,
then,
the audience mainstreams,
programmes, balloons, children carried high,
move as ill-defined cargo,
unsure of where to go.

But the maidens march en-route to mid-day dreams,
knowing that tomorrow, then to face
the battering and buttering,
and switching on machines,
the small routines.

Now is the time for petals in their hair,
Those Neston Ladies walking once a year.

Sylvia Hikins

TIME OUT

Uphill from the tidal saltmarsh
past the new housing estate
I go by bus from Little Neston,
ride to Chester, back in time,
on a dark and rainy summer day;
take refuge in a coffee shop
where burnished wood glows
and silver service gleams.

When I emerge it's summertime
again. I take a boat trip
on the sparkling River Dee where ducks
are dabbling true to form, and in
rear gardens rising from the bank
are *shining ones* whom Betjeman
would love, venturing out to take
afternoon tea on terraces.

I'd like to linger but it's time
for me to take the bus again
to Little Neston; down the hill
through the new housing estate
to the marsh edge where sleepy birds
will sing their bed-time lullabys
to insects and invertebrates —
and look upon rare plants evolved
perhaps from sweepings from grain ships
anchored, heavy laden, on the estuary
of the Dee, where the water's wild
and wide, not Chester-civilised

and time will play its tricks with me
again . . .

Bettina Jones

NESS GARDENS

Months later I return to Ness
Glimpse our once-togetherness
And mourn.
Sunlight on laburnum looms,
Weaves patterns in my head;
Crunching yellow paths
Bound by herbaceous luxury
Hem counterpanes of finest lawn;
Latin-labelled trees from lands
A multitude of miles away
Bring smiles.
How you had teased
My efforts to pronounce!
Burrowing bumble bees
Attracted by a flounce of bluebells
Tuck and gather
Among embroidered heather
Rocked in slumber;
Ring-doves call incessantly
Their parodies of fleeting hours.

I pass serrated panes
Laced with hose for furnishing
Unseasonal rains;
Mitred steps invite —
Below flow crystal threads
Smocking to the lake
Where tadpoles dance,
Dodging delighted childrens'
Drinking cups.
In the wood quiescent creatures
Wait to claim their sovereignty at dusk;
On the seat which
Overlooks the Dee
We once sat reading poetry,
Endeavouring to hold at bay
The closing of our perfect day.

Beguiled by colour,
Scents and sounds
I see us holding hands,
Our souls entwined.
Sadness assuaged
I turn the page —
The Gardens sing renewal.

Valerie M. Carr

QUAKER GRAVES, BURTON
(Inscribed 'The body of Ell-1663 and 7.I.N.l.')

Up grassy paths, beyond Church bounds
two sandstone graves lie out-cast.
No burial in consecrated ground
for this meek Quaker pair, and yet
through sheltering trees
a shaft of falling light
reflects that Inner Light
which filled their lives.

We cannot trace, or time
has hazed their history. Was she 'Ellen',
steadfast in faith
and brave intensity of spirit? Was he 'Nathaniel',
who thought war evil and rejected worship
in 'false temples' with 'false priests'
and sat in silence and listened
to the other voice of God?

Were they persecuted, jailed,
pelted with stones or whipped?
Certain only that they lie
buried on paths where men could tramp
upon their heads, or on their hearts.
Or did they choose this peaceful place
this private plot, away
from the intolerance of man?

Jean Stanbury

A BURTON MANOR COLLAGE

*(a collective poem, written on the Poetry Workshop Course
at Burton Manor College, by the tutor and students)*

A village sloping down towards the Dee —
quiet, thatched remnant of rural society —
here the Manor draws us with nurture of minds.
Screened from the world by sheltering sandstone,
the building's serene, in palladian grace.
Through mahogany doors, brass-lioned,
we come, strengthening our purpose;
soon to sit in cloistered comfort
and let our minds roam free.

Above us, unfingerable Wedgwood, classical relief
in rooms around the chess-board courtyard
where urns hold hyacinths, pink, white, blue.
The wide staircase sweeps us into the past
when couples waltzed over the polished chevrons.
Looking out, we ride with Sir Gawain in the maze
of Wirral woods. Now witch-broom poplars
swish the skyline in a lively breeze
and from the fields, where distant sheep
are patient as unproven dough, comes the smell
of freshmown Spring. The magnolia's trunk
is a question mark: surely its buds will flower,
now encased in green? As if in answer, from crevices
dark and wet, a toad emerges, ambles under leaves,
and golden arrows dart beneath the pond's black lace.

Falling blossoms meet the lawns
as poetry meets our minds.

*Gladys Mary Coles
and poets in her Workshop*

*Elsie Williams, Angela Swann, Joan Reynolds, Norah Mortimer,
Dora Kennedy, Corinne Hedgecock, Pat Sumner, Fay Eagle,
Marjorie Dennison, Gill Cheseldine, Valerie M. Carr, Joan
Bulmer.*

LINES WRITTEN IN BURTON CHURCHYARD

A flag waves triumphantly
from the golden sandstone tower.
Bells clang sonorously,
confetti petals shower
on virginal bride,
pink carnationed groom,
purple decked bridesmaid
and sailor-suited pageboy
standing self-consciously
awaiting the photo ceremonial.

The bridal party leaves
for further festivities.
Bells cease their clanging;
the churchyard empties.

Memory regresses
to a wartime wedding;
no bells by decree,
photographs by brother,
reception by mother,
bridesmaids in borrowed dresses.

We honoured our vows through years which were few.
You left me alone to start life anew.
Time passes, wounds heal,
Life again is sweet.
Pine trees rustle, squirrels scutter,
flowers bloom at my feet.
Hazy mountains, shining river,
squawking gulls intrude,
disperse my dreams.

Away with reminiscing,
leave memories to sleep.
Go out and join the living.

Joan Hartley

THE LIGHT AT INNER MARSH
(Dee Estuary, Burton)

The bird we went for never did appear
Across the fresh lagoons and muddy shore
That opened out below us as we strolled
Down the broad path towards the crowded hide.
Everything seen was commonplace: the tribes
Of gulls; tall waders summer-tinged; sleek grebes.

Yet they were jewels in the tide of light
Which over-the-shoulder flooded in — so bright
It peeled away the dullness from each bird
Till all were miracled, past any word.
A duck's black head, when stroked by wind and sun,
Shimmered dark green as it had never done.

Peter Walton

RIVER VIEWS

At Burton's reeded edge
A wash of birds
Curves from silent towers,
Spurns the sullen river
To follow roads to Wales.
Snow cauls rest on Clwydian hills
Where castles crumble
And the dragon sleeps.

Marjorie Dennison

THE SANDS OF DEE

'O Mary, go and call the cattle home,
  And call the cattle home,
  And call the cattle home,
  Across the sands of Dee.'
The western wind was wild and dank with foam,
  And all alone went she.

The creeping tide came up along the sand,
  And o'er and o'er the sand,
  And round and round the sand,
  As far as eye could see.
The rolling mist came down and hid the land:
  And never home came she.

'Oh! is it weed or fish or floating hair,
  A tress of golden hair,
  A drowned maiden's hair,
  Above the nets at sea?'
Was never salmon yet that shone so fair
  Among the stakes of Dee.

They rowed her in across the rolling foam,
  The cruel, crawling foam,
  The cruel, hungry foam,
  To her grave beside the sea;
But still the boatmen hear her call the cattle home,
  Across the sands of Dee.

Charles Kingsley

Note: Charles Kingsley was a Canon of Chester Cathedral 1870-73. He was inspired to write this poem on seeing a painting by Copley Fielding of the tidal sands and after listening to some old Cheshire stories.

Burton
to
Birkenhead

THE RECUSANT (PUDDINGTON MANOR)

With difficulty,
the Jesuit
clambers up the river bank.
Leather clad feet, stumbling and slewing
on the Mersey mud.
Fingers clawing,
raking the slippery slope.
Heart pounding; breath laboured.
Quiet, essential
sentries on the look-out
for recusants.
King's Orders.

Then suddenly,
the moon,
eclipsed by a veil of cloud,
and shorn of its beams,
aids and abets
his run for shelter.
He makes his bid
and reaches the top.
Black cassock blending with the dark,
he scurries to shelter.
Breathes easy,
sentries unaware.

Puddington Manor
in view.
More than bricks and mortar.
Comfort and sanctuary.
A Jesuit retreat.
Sir Rowland,
friend and benefactor,
waits expectantly.
Confessions, Baptism, Mass,
The Body of Christ,
Soul food,
will cleanse again.

The Wirral,
secret, quiet, benevolent
embraces him.
The Old Religion
will be practised tonight
with heartfelt thanks,
among friends.
Tomorrow, the Dee
will carry him from persecution,
to a land where
God is king,
King not God.

Sandra Kirby

BACKWATER (SHOTWICK)

Hunched in the car, I saw we'd turned
From off the main road down a lane
That led to nowhere, a *via sacra*
Offering a sanctuary from city strain.

Shotwick! When we say Shotwick we can hear
The Norseman sailing up the sheltered creek
To the doomed village, put to fire and sword,
Turning the hamlet to a burning wreck.

Years passed, the Dee ran richly near,
Its waters lapped like lovers the market stone.
Shotwick controlled the crossing of the Dee,
But then, years passed, the tide was blocked,
And the port lay back, an impotent old crone.

For centuries lamps glowed inside the church,
Rosaries slid, altar candles flashed,
Till, by King Henry's law the Latin chant
Was banished, the jewelled windows smashed.

Golf balls and gulls where once the sea had stood,
An ebbed pulsebeat of play and lethargy,
A shell still murmuring when the tide has gone,
As now you doze your sleepwalk life away.

Only one lightning flash of lust
Bursts through the clouds' miscarriaged caul.
William Brereton, gentleman,
Was seized in bed in Shotwick Hall.

They hauled him off to London Town.
He knelt. The steel-cold discipline
Of axe slashed through his neck. He slumped ...
And all for love of Anne Boleyn.

Edward Lloyd

THE CISTERCIAN ABBEY OF STANLOW (STANLAW)
1178-1296 *(Stanlow Point)*

Stanlaw! where I hope to lie
When my hour shall come to die,
Hard thy lot and brief thy fame
Still thou teachest by thy name –
Stan and Law together blending
Name all neighbour names transcending.
Law is hill – I lift my eyes
To the hills beyond the skies.
Stan is Stone – O! Corner Stone!
What art thou but Christ alone?
Altar stone, on thee there lies
That blest Bread of Sacrifice.
Stanlaw! 'tis the Lord above
Gave thy name to tell his love.

13th Century. By an unknown Stanlaw Monk
(trans. from Latin by the Rev. F. G. Slater, Vicar of Ince)

ELLESMERE PORT FROM THE M53

The motorway swoops and curves
across the marshes drained to dreary flatness –
a dyke between town and industrial giants,
glancing the Boat Museum,
where Telford's warehouse stood
when this really was a port.
Now brightly painted narrow boats
and cleaned up brickwork
belie the past. No dirt or bustle,
just sterilised memories jostling
with designer flats and new age artisans.

Cooling towers loom through freezing mist
breathing steam into the curdled sky.
Modern giants in the fake countryside
between Mersey and motorway
facing their symbiotic partner,
the Stanlow oil refinery – spectacular maze
of pipes and structures strung with lights,
crowned by a burning flare.
It's hard to keep your eyes on the road
but the relentless motorway sweeps on
leaving Ellesmere Port behind.

Sue Martin

THE FLY BOAT

Fly boats were specially designed fast narrow boats which, in the 1840s, plied between Ellesmere Port and Birmingham via the Shropshire Union Canal. Travelling day and night, they were timetabled to do the journey in 29 hours leaving Ellesmere Port at 2 o'clock on Monday and Thursday mornings. They specialised in transporting perishable cargo but also took passengers.

Pressing business, Mr Brown?
If you needs must hurry down
To that wilderness of factory, waste and grime:
Yes, the stagecoach is a plague!
But step on board *The Hague*
I'll guarantee to get you there on time.

Me? Captain Smart, I am
Ellesmere Port to Birmingham
We travel there and back, sir, twice a week
Eighty miles or so, each way
You'll arrive there in a day
Both mare and boat are waiting, swift and sleek.

No potholes and no slush
No jumping turnpikes every bumpy mile
No fearful cliffs and canyons
No cheek-by-jowl companions
I promise you, you'll travel, sir, in style.

The train? A troubling notion
Locomotion by explosion;
Just consider the uncertainties of steam
Air thick with coal and cinder
Your beard, sir, likely tinder
Compare that with the pleasures of a stream . . .

Artificial, it is true
But the water flowing through
Might have borne the kings of England on the Thames.
You'll feel regal in a barge
Especially ones as large
As the Shropshire Union's fast and flawless gems.

So you'll join us for the trip?
There's Thomas with his whip
Four times we'll change the horse before we're there.
Loaded down with ore and clay
Every laggard will make way
Nothing dawdling will stop us, I declare.

It's nearly two a.m.
Mantling stars from stern to stem
Stretch your legs beneath the canvas, take your ease
Weather's clear: there's much to see
And to keep you company
Just fifteen tons of ripening Cheshire Cheese.

Alan Davis

THE OLD YEW AT EASTHAM

Now but a shivering husk, a fleshless shell
Whose limbs were old when Norman William ruled;
Its youth long spent when Alfred's Saxon thanes
Did band and fight that England might be freed
From Guthrun's plundering power;
That shaded Werburgh's monks, and watched their church
From mud and wattle change to wood and stone,
And saw Sylvesters come and Stanleys go.
From it the slender longbows came that drove
Their vibrant arrows from the forest's shade
To fill the pot in hovel and in hall,
Or charged the air with death at Agincourt.
So wider spread the ageless, writhing boughs
Reaching to the mellowing walls
Where Warings prayed and Trevors passed to rest
Midst ever-lengthening lanes of daisied mounds
Guarded by bastion stones now moulded green;
Standing like open books to tell the tale
Of all this ancient silent tree has seen.

R. J. Gilpin

from: **AT EASTHAM ON THE MERSEY** (1850s)

... Under green boughs of spreading sycamore
I sit and contemplate this healthful scene,
The woodland scenery skirting either shore
And the broad river stretching far between;
This long green vista, where the elm trees tall,
Embracing, form an archway overhead,
Through which, obliquely, broken sunbeams fall,
And sleep in beauty on the violet's bed.
No sound is heard, save what the wild birds pour,
And ripples gushing on the rocky shore.

Richard Crompton
Note: *Richard Crompton, Liverpool poet and editor of*
'Liverpool Lantern', was a friend of Charles Dickens.

EASTHAM LOCKS

In the quiet of the night you'd hear the sound
  of ships at Eastham locking.
The sound of the tugs would echo round
  the channel with them docking.
Point Linas pilots' skills had brought
  the ships into the river.
From here they'd work to Salford Quays
  their cargoes to deliver.

What seas they'd travelled oceanwide,
  the many ports they'd entered.
What cargoes stored within the holds
  from countries where they'd ventured.
Each funnel showed the shipping line
  with owners' designation
And on the stern for all to see
  the port of registration.

And into Queen's Dock there would come
  some quite astounding tankers
Of new and elegant designs
  all owned by rich Greek bankers.
The barges, coasters and small craft
  which travelled up the Weaver,
Would also navigate the locks
  as busy as a beaver.

Then down would come the same fine ships
  with new industrial cargoes,
All safely towed from Manchester
  through locks to meet the tide-flows.
The smoke-stacks were re-fitted by
  the giant crane on the lockside.
And busy crews were working with
  the warps along the tugs' side.

Containers now have changed the course
  of this old institution,
With giant tankers — Tranmere based —
  have brought a revolution.
The distant sound of whistles which
  resounded round the Mersey,
Have faded with the sound of steam
  and days which seemed more carefree.

Philip Bastow

DIBBINSDALE

O those long-lost bluebell Sundays,
Those green tunnels in the wood.
When dragons stalked behind the trees
And life was still in bud.

O those long-lost bluebell Sundays,
Those mailed horsemen by the lake;
And the din of ancient battle
And so many paths to take.

O those long-lost bluebell Sundays;
Cannot you see them just ahead?
O lead me gently to my childhood,
Let the green fern be my bed.

John Reynolds

POULTON HALL (1939)

There is a place that to my private view
More hallowed is than Athens or than Rome:
An English house it is, an English home,
Dark oaks against the sky's September blue,
Green lawns, lush meadows, fields of Autumn's hue
The violet hills beneath the setting sun
The stage where life's first course for me was run.

Dear for itself, and holy in my sight,
At once the fount and goal of my desires;
Here thirty generations of my sires
Trod the same paths, beneath the same sun's light;
And I come after, strengthened for life's fight
By their endeavours – may I go my way
From dawn to eve worthy to be as they.

Roger Lancelyn Green

THE GHOST OF POULTON HALL

The wind blows cold in Dibbinsdale,
Driving thick snow in powdered cliffs drifting
Over the roadway, down to the frozen river.
Fearful the deep woods rising sheer in ragged moonlight,
Lonely the figure stumbling upwards,
Lifting her long skirts high in icy fingers,
Glint of gold ring, Bride of Christ,
Anxiously glancing now and then at the coach below,
Wedged on the hump-backed bridge,
Breath from the horses rising, her sisters waiting.

A lantern swings in the brewhouse yard
As she passes by; snow on the barrels,
Latch to the gloom beyond, a stench of hops steeping;
No-one about but a cat asleep on sacking heaped
In a cobweb corner. Only a curious barn owl sees
As she slips through trees at the hill-top's edge,
To tug on the bell-rope hung in the porch
Of Poulton Hall.

Within, the wolfhounds whine and pace
As windows shake, and down the chimney
Melted snowflakes drip and hiss on dying embers.
Lord of the Manor, sprawled at table, raises his eyes
To the girl before him, shivering wet
In a whisper speaking; beckons her closer,
Softly smiling, watches her white face – terror dawning.
Swiftly she turns as he reaches forward,
Runs for her soul down dim-lit passages,
White veil flying, Mother of God . . .
In through an archway, scent of leather,
Books to the ceiling, crouch in shadow; football, door slam,
Click of a key; poor little nun in the darkness weeping,
Praying for strength to keep her vows; pity her sisters
Huddled, waiting – they'll not arrive at the Priory tonight –
And she never will.

Heather Wilson

THE BATTLE OF BRUNANBURH, 937

King Athelstan, the lord of warriors,
Patron of Heroes, and his brother too,
Prince Edmund, won themselves eternal glory
In battle with the edges of their swords
Round Brunanburh; they broke the wall of shields . . .
      . . . There the Norseman's chief
Was put to flight, and driven by dire need
With a small retinue to seek his ship
The ship pressed out to sea, the King departed
Onto the yellow flood and saved his life . . .

*Extract from the Old English poem The Battle of Brunanburh
selected by Richard Hamer in* A Choice of Anglo-Saxon Verse
(1970)

*The Battle of Brunanburh, AD 937, fought between the West
Saxon King Athelstan and Edmund, his brother, against Anlaff,
Norse King of Northumbria and his combined forces of Welsh
princes, Scots, Irish and Vikings, is thought to have taken place at
Bromborough alongside the Mersey (the 'yellow flood' on which
Anlaff fled?).*

SEA-CHANGE AT BROMBOROUGH

Yesterday...
I walk my dog across the open field
The short grass ripples
mimics mighty Mersey's ruffled face
Gulls rest here
seek refuge from the flowing tide
Longer grasses toss the fretful moth
and energetic bee clings to the breeze
The smell of mudflat merges
with the scent of shrubs and trees
cooling the summer haze
A flash of black and white
denotes our Dolly's tail
zigzags across the sea of wavy grass
Nose submerged unearths the rabbit's trail
four miles upstream
from Woodside ferry

Today...
I leave the dog penned in the car
The virgin turf mown down impassive
conforms to civilised convention
reflects the harshness of the Chester Road
No longer may the moth just laze
no pollen tempts the reckless bee
and yet
the gulls still seek a haven here
like refugees in no-man's land
Black seas of tarmac spread
bake in the summer heat
solidify the earth
White lines shimmer
state where cars may wait
in the fume-filled air
No rabbits run
Workers toil in tin-box units
windowless but dry
deaf to every sea-gull's cry
Sunday shoppers trundle trolleys
around the tin-box superstore

Lovers cling and laugh
make merry
in tin-box pub and club
seek to stem time's flowing tide
four miles upstream
from the ferry
at Woodside

Gordon Thompson

WORSHIP ANCIENT AND MODERN

Wheatfield tall, dry, yellowed, ripe for harvest,
Soft autumn winds blow gentle, bend all ears in unison,
Rippling grassy vision like an ocean, hypnotic movement,
Distant hedgerow pruned by weathered fingers, cuts the land.
A small perhaps intended break in the hedge, forms a frame,
Mystic picture of two cathedrals, outlined in one small square.

Clear image of ancient and modern as if preconceived,
The architect had planned some secret symmetry,
They point heavenward together. This unexpected scene
Recalls a place where stones have stood long and silent,
On sites specially selected to align with the Sun God,
Mathematically engineered, and still fascinating
Captivating the minds and hearts of men.

Linda Bradley

Note: *Written after a walk across Bromborough Golf
Course, looking at the two Liverpool Cathedrals.*

SPITAL CROSSROADS

Down Church Road, then round the bend,
There you will find Four Lanes End.
That was its name years ago —
Back then, for a day trip, families would go
All the way to Raby Mere
Not to Blackpool or Wigan Pier.
Spital Cross Roads is its nearly new name,
I'm sad to say it's not the same.
I wish once more that it could be
Not shops or pubs but field and tree.
Those trees stood grandly, green and tall,
But roads and car fumes destroyed it all.
For this terrible act, man takes the blame,
I, for one, think it's a great shame.
But one thing remains from history,
The sheep-pen fold, so very old,
Still stands strong for all to see.

Laura Plested
(age 11 yrs)

The Chirotherium - this dinosaur lived 200 million years ago on the muddy sand of the desert area around what is now the river Mersey and its shores. Sets of prints were found in sandstone slabs at Storeton Quarries, Wirral, in 1838. Chirotherium is known as the 'Hand Animal'.

BEBINGTON CHURCH

Nixon's Prophecy:
When that spire's vane shall clasp
Ivy with its fatal grasp,
Then the last stern trumpet's call,
Live and dead shall summon all.
Then shall hap the crash of doom,
Then the dead shall burst the tomb,
Together crushed the world shall roll,
Like the parched flame-shrivelled scroll.

Many years since then have passed,
Still the world and spire last;
Nor yet the ivy's fatal grasp
Dares the fatal point to clasp.
Once it almost reached the height,
Filling Cheshire with affright;
When the lightning's scorched blast
Through the threatening ivy passed.
Twice since then in utmost need,
Chance has baulked the ivy's greed;
Still the tendrils seek the sky,
Struggling towards the spire on high.

Egerton Leigh

STORETON

Evening in the woods at Storeton
And a late bird flies startled along the tilting path
And pines step carefully down into the shadows by the ditch
And in the adjoining field the rabbits are dispersing.

Then darkness moves swiftly in across the hedgerows
And all at once the world is out of reach
beyond the circling curtain of the wood

And I have watched too long
And look in vain for the farmhouse lights over Barnston way.

John Reynolds

PORT SUNLIGHT VILLAGE

A footprint on the sands of history,
erased by a brush of desert wind,
is an average sort of legacy for most:
but Lever left a Utopian dream drawn from a marsh.
A place for his workers,
escape from tumbledown squalor,
space for limbs to stretch and breathe.
Nothing missing from the grand design,
guiding each stage of the human journey.
Entry to life and health in his hospital,
nurturing young minds in the school.
His church marks the station of their lives,
outside, a garden of eternal rest.

The factory toils in scented harmony,
clattering out supplies for the world.
A one-man anti-grime campaign,
shaped, stamped, wrapped, despatched,
by rail and road to the towns, to the ports,
mass-produced, promoted, projected,
all in the cause of cleaning mankind.

A short walk from the cloying sweetness,
past the well-groomed gardens,
an architectural cocktail, a planned heaven.
At the heart, a treasured temple,
cradled alabaster against a horizon of roses.
Inside, his elegant choice,
revealing his feel for the art of his age.
Tender remembrance for a lifetime's companion,
colours, textures, moods and shapes;
escape into a Pre-Raphaelite dream
with Holman Hunt, Rossetti and Millais.

Gently back along the roses,
the patch-work of structures,
half-timber, red brick and grey stone.
Easy to murmur, "Nice, isn't it."
But to me, total wonderment:
one man's vision of work and life.

Robin Thomas

THE VILLAGE

Cheeky cherub blowing bubbles
watches as they rise
reflecting rainbows
in a rich man's eyes.

Tall twisted chimneys
and Rapunzel towers
crown houses built by dreamers
in green pastures
where children play
and dogs are walked
on tree-lined paths.

Water softly falls,
a glittering arch
rising from iron horse
with fish and men entwined;
a fountain fills the centre ground
while soldiers frozen in relief
keep faith with memories
of war and peace.

Above it all stands Christ
set on a pinnacle of stone,
all-seeing, all forgiving
and alone.

In the Gallery
proud and virile Greek gods pose
for dreaming beauties
by Pre-Raphaelites
while Nelson's Emma Hamilton
still dances with her tambourine.

From cleanliness to godliness
And dolly-tub to blue rinse,
here factory, school and church
fed bodies, minds and souls
of people bathed in sunlight
and sheltered by strong walls.

Sheila Parry

THE LADY LEVER ART GALLERY

Two poems for paintings in the Gallery

1. *The Scapegoat, William Holman Hunt, 1854*

*And the Goat shall bear upon him all the iniquities unto a land
not inhabited. (Leviticus xvi 22)*

This goat's a ragged beast
his harmless horns bound with scarlet –
they wreathed him in red on Atonement Day
to carry away their sins, bear the stain.
Now, goaded into this wilderness, he stands
desolate on the Dead Sea shore.
Almost sinking in the sand, as if weighed down
by a cross, he stumbles, thirst-racked
near the salt water, tideless sea of Sodom.

Will his scarlet turn to white
signifying sins forgiven? Not until
his bones whiten the white sand
and his bleached garland is time's token.

Gladys Mary Coles

2. The Kelpie, Herbert Draper, 1913

Kelpy (Gaelic): A fabled spirit reputed to haunt lakes and rivers delighting in the drowning of travellers and others. (O.E.D.)

Some words do not translate:
they do not exist in English.
One tongue slips through the other's grasp,
ignoring our clear divisions
of green from blue, blue from grey.
But hidden in the Gaelic are other hues,
shades we do not see.
And as in the *gaeltacht* the light refracts anew,
so the boundaries of the visible
and the invisible are different here.
The blind have been seers;
sight defies the eyes.

He, a painter in this alien spectrum, learned this,
drawn from his familiar colours
into light broken and rewoven
his eyes ceased to resist, and so
he crossed that rift in subtle sense
that holds the worlds apart
and keeps us sane.

Faithful, he painted what he saw,
what could not be there.
At the pool of *glas allt*
an elemental spirit watching by the water,
Kelpie
knowing the word true.

Edmund Cusick

Allt – a stream.
Glas – grey, blue, or green (the correspondence with the English spectrum is only partial)
Gaeltacht – that area within which Gaelic is spoken as the first language.

CERAMICS
(The Lady Lever Art Gallery)

From an original mould
   rare bowls
   on show in subdued light
   inner hollow . . . old designs
   surfaces and solid bases chased
   like chalices. Art and informed mind
   transient as sand in glass.

   Figures – attic black
chariots carrying ancient gods
bard, dancer beating tambourine
already moving onward through perspective
but only around the arena
of a vase
where visions of elysian fields
are grounded in arcadian clay
as laurels of philosophy and sophistry decay.

   Figures – gold on Ming
at leisure in a landscape of high pine
silk roads wild with peonies
lead only to the lip
of a jar of wine.
Immortal sweetmeats
peach-bloom, pomegranate seed
in slow motion shattering to shards
as Sung and Ming and Manchu dragons starve.

   Figures – Wedgwood white
a long and ghostly human frieze
populations raised . . . for a repository
a bon-bon pot
and monumental funerary urn.
Enduring enigmas hardly change.
   Who is the potter, pray, and who the pot?
Why deft hands are still demanding,
using new machines,
treasure from dust?

                                     Gina Riley

ROCK FERRY AFTERNOON

In the main shopping street,
Just on the corner,
They gather together,
Prams spreading out in a circle,
Impeding passers-by.

There's tall ones, small ones,
Fat ones, thin ones:
Short skirts, long skirts,
Pony tails, blonde scrunches,
Limpid locks. No wedding rings.

And the babies:
Some lying, dummies in,
Some crying, dummies out.
Bottles draining, prams shaking.
Kisses, scolding.

The girls light up their cigarettes;
Exchange troubles,
Laughing, confiding;
Shouting farewells
As they head for home.

Back to their rooms, flats, tenements.
Child mums, seemingly unaware
Of missing out on teenage years.
Not sad. Not bad. No enormity.
Something to love is security.

Jean Lewis

IN ROCK PARK

Dilapidated now, prostituted,
The Georgian mansion, standing four-square
Above the river, in the once exclusive park;

In the lofty first-floor drawing room
The spirit of the old sea captain gazes
Mournfully over the empty river.

The ghost of his Lady regards
The patch of neglected lawn below;
All that remains of her splendid garden
Is the Japanese tree, bare,
Wrinkled and twisted, with weeping downward fingers.

She looks sourly askance at the rough men
In faded jeans and dusty woollen hats
Working where her flowers once grew,
Drinking beer beside their upturned dinghies
And battered sailing craft.

But her husband drifts happily among these latter-days
Signalling their heady perfume of varnish,
Gristling away with sand-paper;
He understands their longing, their imagining,
Their flight from office desks,
From cramping wife and kids:

The faraway look in the yachtsmen's eyes
Is reflected in his own.

Mary Brett

ROCK PARK

At night,
the sky tumbles towards
the edge of the world.
While towards the beach
houses hold themselves safe,
tall and gaunt.
Faded windows, eyes to the past,
like wounds left bleeding.
In need of care
they wait for attention
and in the distance
light flickers
on the lacquered oil terminal
defiling the view.
A sign of the present.
While old boats lie dying
they act as a reminder
and in the November wind
the toll gates creak and shudder
waiting for you to pass through.
While in the Old Admiral
voices can be heard
failing on the wind
like old ghosts dancing.

Barbara Hope Allan

Nathaniel Hawthorne, the
American Consul in Liverpool,
lived at 26 Rock Park 1853-56.

TRANMERE BASEMENT BLUES

In our little home from home before the war,
Where sunlight seldom finds a chink,
Cockroaches caper creepily on the floor
And slimy slugs slide sinuously round the sink.

Beneath the gaslamp's yellow light,
Rain shimmers on the endless street.
Steam trains toil slowly in the night,
And from the foggy river, sirens call.

Smart in his pinstripe suit and two-tone feet,
Clark Gable goes out to the billiard hall,
Leaves Greta Garbo waiting by her radio,
All dressed up once more, and nowhere left to go.

Douglas Griffiths

POLLING STATION

Tranmere Higher Grade School (St. Andrew)

The rooms that once
seemed vast,
Where grown-ups seemed immensely tall,
Are small.
That is the first impression.
The second is the smell
Of ink and chalk,
Wood polish and the fresh-scrubbed floor.

All these combine
To form a picture of the school
From earliest Infants memories, the phoney war
When nothing happened
Except for gas mask drill.
Evacuation schemes, the blitz,
The shattered windows hanging on the tape,
Unexplained empty desks.
All the paraphernalia of war,

Buckets and candles, make do and mend.
Dig for Victory, which came eventually,
And the sudden sense of being big
And moving on.

'Place your vote in the box, please,
And hand your card in by the door.'

Douglas Griffiths

When gorse is in blossom and holly is green,
Prenton Hall Buggon is then to be seen.

Buggon - Ghost   *Old Rhyme*

57600 (Prenton, 1947)

It's Monday: Mum will take her to the shops
On Woodchurch Road: to Waterworth's, where once
She spat out a banana, hard and green
Straight off the boat from Ffyffe's – a special treat:
The first one seen in Prenton since the War;
    To the Co-op, with sawdust on the floor:
    Soft wsssh of bacon-slicer on the left,
    White sugar in blue packets to the right,
    And tea – four ounces: here's the Ration Book.
    Share-number, luv? Five-seven-six-oh-oh . . .
And can we go and feed the ducks?

On Friday, get the 77 bus
To Charing Cross, and wander down Grange Road
With Mum in dark green coat with nipped-in waist
(For no-one can avoid Dior's New Look),
But don't set foot in Robb's: it's far too posh.
    Go into Woolworth's, Marks and Spencer, Boots,
    Then to the big Co-op department store
    And watch, wide-eyed, the brass pneumatic tubes
    Whoosh pounds and pence and 57600
    To some unfathomed place of reckoning . . .
Collect the divi, and go home for tea.

I. H. Hanson

INSIDE THE WILLIAMSON ART GALLERY

Beyond the Ionian pillars, the men
In uniform. Behind a velvet cord
The old cars sleep, their years of driving done.
A bull-nosed Morris with its brass unflawed,
And there, behind, a Jowett Javelin,
Still elegant as a blue chinchilla cat,
Pleading for a hand to pet
Its slanting curves, to coax its engine
To a sewing machine hum, 53 b.h.p.
Tiny yet with verve you took me
From Calabar to Enugu through viscous mud
Clogging the wheels in tendrils of brown froth,
Skirting Cross River's fly-plagued bed,
Your seat a band of sweat-soaked cloth.

Beyond the cars I move into
A plush Victorian world, where paintings roam
The walls. One holds me as I pause below
Its message. A girl stands by a tomb.
Near her, her father tears his snow-white hair,
Sinks down, half paralysed with grief,
His hands outstretched towards the grave.
They are an ill-assorted pair.
Mourning becomes the girl, it tears
the man in two. And now for both, the years
Have signed their autograph of dust,
And on the painter too. The name
Spells 'ending' shaded beyond the frame.
I leave the opium warmth for winter's robust
Light. Who knows? I may yet have two years or thrice
To wash the years away like lice,
And keep my brain from catching rust.

Edward Lloyd

FOR THE CENTENARY OF WILFRED OWEN (1893-1918)

The sea is rising . . . and the world is sand
                                        – Wilfred Owen, 1916

In Milton Road tonight, a boy playing in the summer light
wears a crash helmet, manoeuvres his bike.
Down the slope he rides, shoots a frown at me,
aware that I'm staring at Fifty-One –
Victorian villa, the Birkonian home
of the Owens (Tom, Susan, four children).
From here Wilfred, proud of his uniform,
smartly set off to Whetstone Lane and school.
A time that was nurturing, unriven:
Sunday School at Claughton, walks to Bidston –
woods and windmill he knew well; also Meols
(his cousins' house 'Dorfold'). For young Harold
brotherly protection, inventions, games.
And boyhood joys – swimming at local Baths,
riding a horse beside wild Mersey waves;
his pleasure in learning, crafting first poems.

Ten years from here, a lifetime further on,
nerves shattered by shell-fire near St. Quentin,
did he, perhaps, think back to Birkenhead,
recall the mothering hours at Milton Road
where a boy, tonight, is riding his bike in the summer light.

                                        Gladys Mary Coles

*Wilfred Owen spent seven formative years in Birkenhead where
he attended Birkenhead Institute (1900-1907). His father was
Assistant Station Master at Woodside GWR Station. The Owens
lived at 7 Elm Grove (which bears an English Heritage plaque),
14 Willmer Road and 51 Milton Road.*

BIRKENHEAD PRIORY IN 1777
from: Mount Pleasant

Far on the view – at soften'd distance seen,
Whilst rolls the stream its copious waves between,
There – long deserted by the sable band,
A lonely abbey glooms upon the strand:
When once the towering arch, in Gothic state
Rose high; and frown'd recluse the iron grate:
But shook by time, the lofty columns fall
The wide roof drops, and sinks the mouldering wall;
The hollow gale thro' every cavern flies,
And the dull owl repeats her midnight cries.

William Roscoe

The seal of Birkenhead Priory.

BIRKENHEAD PRIORY, 1819

The pointed arch, divested of its door,
The broken staircase and disjointed floor,
The fractured wall, on which its wild flower blooms,
The lancet windows, and monastic rooms –
Are objects dear to contemplation's view:
In them she traces charms forever new.
And thence departs with an unsated zest,
As quits a pensive bird its plundered nest.

Thomas Whitby

BIRKENHEAD PRIORY
Founded circa 1150 by Hamo de Massey

Hemmed in by industry
this place of prayer survives the centuries.
Through each stone arch
shadows seem peopled by blackrobed monks
their quiet lives ordered
by the sun's rising and its set.

'Laborare est orare' – service to their God
and man. Fishermen, farmers, ferrymen,
a royal right in perpetuity
to ferry travellers
across the clear waters of the bay
from silvery headland of oak and birch.

Dissolution – a long descent into decay,
a pensioned Prior, a wandering of monks,
a passing to oblivion
of those quiet times. Yet myths persist,
a secret passage, entombed monks
buried alive with Priory gold.

Regeneration – discoveries,
a Prior's grave, a golden noble, wild boar's tusk.
Children clatter a spiral staircase
spy through peepholes, hope for ghosts.
Visitors linger, study the handprints of history,
absorb the peace.

Jean Stanbury

THE CHILDREN'S GRAVEYARD

Sheltered by Priory walls,
grassed over now, this bone-ridden plot.
A few small lozenges survive
pitted by lichen, mute testimony
to high mortality in harsher times.

Victorian sorrows – for 'Wee George
your Father bids you home'; twin graves
a daughter and a son, 'Louise and James'
then earlier still just names remain
'Our Bertie', 'Paddy', 'Little Ned'.

Impossible in later years to visualize
in that flat ground such mounds of misery,
massed tragedy beneath our feet.
This peaceful solitude, where monks once walked
seems stained with sorrow.

Jean Stanbury

THE OPENING OF BIRKENHEAD DOCKS, 1847
(Song)

Come, heave ahead boys,
Come heave ahead,
And throw the dock gates open for the ships of Birkenhead,
Then Birkenhead will smile,
And ships from every isle,
Will sail into the harbour, in a very little while.
Then comes the happy day
When anchored in the bay,
With ships a building on the stocks, preparing for the sea,
Come heave ahead boys,
Come heave ahead.

Lord Morpeth will come down boys,
Lord Morpeth will come down,
To Birkenhead with gentlemen and ladies of renown,
Will dress the Mayor's fool,
That resides in Liverpool,
When he comes to Birkenhead to learn the golden rule.
On April the fifth,
Each boat will sail adrift,
The flag of honour and free trade in Birkenhead we'll lift.

What a day for fun boys,
What a day for fun,
The merchants of great Liverpool 'twill give them such a stun,
The gates will open wide,
The free and rolling tide,
Will flow into the splendid dock, that's to open at Woodside.
The commissioners, you'll see,
They will all so happy be,
With a roaring trade in Birkenhead, and sweet prosperity.

The ships are on the stocks boys,
The ships are on the stocks,
Jolly tars in Birkenhead will assemble now in flocks.
The ladies they can wed,
In Woodside and Birkenhead,
And they'll have no occasion to be toiling for their bread.
The ships from near and far

And each jolly roving tar,
And ladies wearing bustles like a British Man o' War.

The nation we'll surprise boys,
The nation we'll surprise
To see the grand warehouses for holding merchandise.
The work that's now complete
Is nothing to relate
And what you'll see in Birkenhead upon a future date,
Warehouses in a throng,
Streets seventeen miles long,
The Birkenhead commissioners will sing a merry song.

Birkenhead does rise boys,
Birkenhead does rise,
And the day is fast approaching when the world will see
The splendid market place
Beef and mutton to embrace,
A splendid park in Birkenhead, to ramble at your ease
The shipping in galore
Will fill the dock and more,
Plenty of work, and wages good, will crown the shore.

(Song sung in Birkenhead Park, 1847)

MORPETH DOCK, BIRKENHEAD

The squalls that blew the cattle boat from Dublin
dashed themselves out with impotent fury on the Mersey Bar
And all is calm.

In Morpeth Dock, the flaring gas-light draws
Steam from a thousand sunken flanks.
Sick yellow eyes roll mournfully and vermin hop and creep
In filthy straw about their hooves.

Along the quay, a power-house belches flame,
Goods-wagons clank and groan
And engines shriek into the station roof,
Looming like Lucifer over everlasting fire.

The ramps are lowered now and drovers swarm the decks
Belabouring the cattle viciously with knotted sticks.
They swing their massive heads in sad bewilderment
Thinking their torments had been at an end – and one by one
They stumble down the ramps,
Now crashing to their bony knees, now struggling upright,
Lowing, in misery, shying from the whips.

Dry land at last – but then another ramp –
A tortuous tunnel, swooping black above the docks,
Smelling of fear and trampled excrement of bygone herds,
Who made their long journey from the hills of Ireland
To death.

Heather Wilson

PEOPLE'S CARRIAGE
(Birkenhead, August 30th 1860)

New tentacles of steel reached to the park
from Woodside Ferry, waiting the first car.
Familiar sound of hoof on road combined
with grind of wheel on rail as trams rolled by.

George Francis Train, American and loud,
brought People's Carriages from Baltimore
to Birkenhead, a pioneering town,
to give trams their first foothold on our shores.

Five thousand rode that first day through the throng,
men back to back upstairs, ladies inside.
Tram horses worked in pairs to haul their loads
of up to forty people through the town.

Today, new trams at Woodside greet the crowds.
Made in Hong Kong to ply for tourist trade,
they carry pleasure-seekers back to times
when Birkenhead was thriving, Cheshire's pride.

Malcolm Chisholm

THE LAST LAUNCHING

Glass into a thousand fragments smashed,
fruits of Mother Nature
flowed down the man-made vessel's side.
Quietly, she slipped serenely
into muddy Mersey waters,
sequel to Great Ships of War.
Hooting tugs and yachts
welcomed her afloat.
Black metal shimmering in the April sun.

Men stood with pride.
They cheered and doffed their caps and
waved their woolly hats.
Was it tears or
salt spray from the sea
that trickled down weathered faces –
to touch their lips?
Along with children's voices,
they sang . . .
'Abide with me.'

Skilful fingers had
humoured her with each caress,
as a perfect body moulded.
She was a goddess. Supreme . . .
their daily manna.
Ghosts of years past
were scattered amongst unbelieving crowds
waving Union Jacks.

She would be leaving soon
for distant waters.
Men looked on
with sadness in their aching hearts –
as they saw lifeblood and sweat
ebbing away with the tide.

'H.M.S. UNICORN'

Anne Green

EPITAPH TO CAMMELL LAIRD

Silence sits upon
empty slipways.
The launch of a gull
into flight brings
no cheering crowds.
Wooden wedges, which
held leviathans in check,
now bedecked with seaweed,
encrusted with barnacles,
are tossed aside
like playthings of
Neptune's child.
Rusted drag chains
lie coiled in a
Daedalian heap.
The river swashes idly
into empty docks.
Footsteps of the
solitary watchman echo
with a hollow ring.

Sandra Kirby

TALKING NEWSPAPER

Every week
yellow wallets speed
from studios down deep
in the building that was once
Birkenhead Children's Hospital
to many parts of Wirral.

Every week
into someone's home
chattering cassettes come
to combat isolation as
familiar voices greet
people they seldom meet.

Every week
from Bebington to Irby,
when one sense has ceased to be
and life threatens to contract,
a net is spread out that tries
to catch events with friendly eyes.

Peggy Poole

THE NEW SHOPPING MALL

The doors swing open and in we go.
It's warm in here: there is no snow.
The ceiling is high and when I look up,
Is that a chandelier I see?
Surely not in this modern setting
Of famous chains and discount shoes,
Of cafeterias and spotless loos . . .
It's all so pleasant:
No elements intrude.

But what is this sigh for?
Do I wish to turn back?
To when along the High Street we'd go,
In the cold and the snow
To the butcher and shoemaker and on to the baker
Whose pervading aromas – hot coffee and rolls,
Warmed our souls.

Jean Lewis

THE THEATRE GHOST (Birkenhead, The Little Theatre)
(Macbeth. Scene IV, The Palace.
First murderer concealed ready to enter)

Unseen, I hear their voices on the stage.
Silent I wait, a harbinger of death.
With inner eye I scan the scripted page
The cue for me to seek my Lord Macbeth.

The audience, a dark pulsating beast,
Anticipates the human sacrifice.
Lost, out of joint, I join the Scottish feast.
An empty stage? Within an empty space?

With Banquo's blood upon my face, I plead
With strangers – see me, I am here!
Banquo is dead, for I've done the deed.
Which I must report, so I pray do not fear.

No harm is meant when I stand here with you.
The years have passed by as I wait for my cue.

Don McLean

THE BLACK CHAIR OF BIRKENHEAD

An Ode to Hedd Wyn (1887-1917)

Not in green Wales this Eisteddfod,
the National 1917 in soot-dark Birkenhead.
Far from your mountain moors, Trawsfynydd,
the clear streams, sweet river Prysor,
flock, farm and family –
yet not so far as Passchendaele.

That September the trees in the Park
were already leafed in red
when from the stage your name was called,
the heraldic call across the massive tent,
a ritual summons to claim the bardic prize.
Archdruid Dyfed, Lloyd George, Leverhulme, knew
from that audience you would not rise.

The empty Chair enveloped in black,
your absence filling the auditorium
told of Armageddon
as you lay in Flanders, six weeks dead.

Given into your family's keeping
the dark-draped throne on a cart
was processed the long lane to Yr Ysgwrn.
Crested with flaring dragons
its fine oak craftsman-carved
by a Belgian refugee of Borough Road.

Gladys Mary Coles

Hedd Wyn was the Bardic name of Ellis Humphrey Evans of Trawsfynydd, Merionethshire, killed in France, 31 July 1917 in the Third Battle of Ypres (Passchendaele).
The Royal National Eisteddfod, 2-9 September 1917, was held in Birkenhead Park. Hedd Wyn won the Chair with his awdl (ode) on the set theme 'The Hero'.
The Chair was carved by Mr Van Fleteran of Malines, Belgium, a refugee then living in Borough Road, Birkenhead.

BIRKONIAN CHILDHOOD

On corners we played, darting
In and out of evening shadows,
Swinging thin bodies
In tangle of sturdy rope
Snaking around street lamps.

The market place bellowed its own special sounds.
Traders, rattling cups, juggling plates,
Called their wares to evening strollers.

Further along the river-front Toc H glowed
Sailor's refuge, within earshot of anvils striking
Pom-pom's riveting, arc 'n' arc sparking,
Great ships shuddering.

Doris Lamount

BIRKENHEAD PARK

Early morning mists of Autumn
Ebbing palely in the park
And the port-hole sun arising
Pierces through the failing dark.

Stray patrols of press-ganged schoolboys
Crab their way across the paths
And a washed-up cat lies stretching
On the bench's broken laths.

Now I see the leaves like pebbles
And the sea-weed grass laid bare
Then a bird high in the crows-nest
Cries along the shining air.

John Reynolds

HAMILTON SQUARE HAIKU

Laird's impressive Square
Creamy Storeton stone houses
Formal flower gardens.

Laird's statue sees change
Now elegant offices
Lunch-hours with flowers.

Alan Stanbury

HAMILTON SQUARE

The green-hatted clock of the Town Hall tower
Chimed our childhood hours away
Dictating our lives as it tolled every quarter
A quickening of feet, a distraction of thoughts.

The square is encircled by dowager queens
Their souls set in stone, like lawyers in judgment.
Window boxes like overgrown eyebrows
Stand with their backs to the surroundings.

Clothed in ivy, clinging tight
A hint of colour, a touch of life,
This plant is witness to times gone by
When the horse-drawn carriage was a regular sight.

Old men slumber in Summertime
On benches warmed by the heat of the day,
A halting place for the Silver Prize Band,
Their shining brasses reflecting the sun.

I've played on the up-and -over steps
Raced along the criss-cross paths
Skirted the railings of manicured lawns
Surrounding Queen Victoria's Cake.

On the western side John Laird looks down;
With hawk-like eye he studies the changes.
Pomaded and cleansed as a new born babe,
He smilingly fingers his beardless chin.

Kathleen Dhenin

THE MERSEY RAILWAY

The smoke, the soot, the noise, the smell.
Commuters rode through Dante's hell
beneath the River Mersey's bed
from Liverpool to Birkenhead.

When storm and fog kept ferries tied
to landing stages either side
no railway passenger turned back.
Trains always ran along this track.

Electric trains replaced the steam.
The air was fresh, the stations clean.
They sped beneath the waves and through
the Cheshire countryside they flew.

Now Merseyrail, where counties merge,
links north and south beneath the surge.
New trains and tunnels loop their way
through roots and dreams of yesterday.

Malcolm Chisholm

RETURNING TO HAMILTON SQUARE STATION

The subterranean capsule
sucks walls, travelling at speed
through darkness, clinging to bends
like the frightened in panic
fleeing from something
larger than themselves.

Inside, frayed commuters slouch
on seats, pale green check,
the tartan of an ailing clan;
they pretend to ignore each other,
uneasy, they are spies at windows
eavesdropping to pass the time.

Together, train and tunnel,
one large grumbling intestine,
transport passengers
into the washroom-white
of the underground station,
as brakes emit a twisted scream.

Spewed from open-mouthed doors,
travellers re-group, mobilise;
take direction from little green men
that run along walls, up escalators,
their agile guides in case of fire.

They file into metal cabinets
caged for the trip to the surface;
'Stand clear, doors closing',
says the electronic voice;
everyone smiles, someone giggles,
they study their feet, and rise.

Miriam Bennett

HISTORIC WARSHIPS

H.M.S. Plymouth; Onyx a German U-boat –
    retired from conflict.
Open for visits, on the Mersey's western shore,
    all lie, respected.
From different sides, these hunters, fighters, killers
    in different wars.

Weapons, cramped spaces, exhort us to visualize
    the reality –
on different sides, *men*, fighting, killing, drowning.
    Indifferent War.

Hilary Tinsley

from: **SHIPS**

Some people on Wirral wake to the song of birds –
the ubiquitous blackbird has no class preference,
he'll share his avine aria with anyone
(providing there's a cat-free tree at the back of your house).

Some people on Wirral look out of their windows
onto stretches of seaside,
the Welsh mountains (when the light is good),
or pretty gardens with variegated plants.

But to go to your front door for the milk
or to pick up the post,
when a thin, damp, lung-tickling mist
squats like a broody hen on the pavement,
and cats are just starting to patrol
their morning beat on backyard walls,

and see, indistinctly, in the half-light,
looming above the bitumastic-black sheds of Vittoria dock,
hovering over the edge of your street – a SHIP!
the topmasts, derrick-riggings, the Reckitt's blue funnel
of a China boat, flying light –
that is really something to write home about.

Gus Halligan

THE STRONG SALT WINDS AT LIVERPOOL

The strong winds at Liverpool
   That sweep across the Bay
Once brought the great proud ships of old
   With teak from Mandalay,
With bars of gold from lands untold
   With cloves from Zanzibar,
With tea and jute from Chittagong
   And rubber from Para;
Trim figure-head and snowy sail,
   Tall mast and tapered spar,
A rhythmic shanty from the waist,
   The smell of Stockholm tar.

And ugly ducklings plough and sheer
   Where once there sailed a swan.

John E. M. Sumner

SOMERSAULT

Pearly girly, coming for a twirly
   Over on the railings by the landing quarter,
Whirly-curly, see the hurly-burly
   Early from the ferry dirling over Mersey water.

Furling on the railings, waving to the sailings,
   Tug boat, pilot cutter, Cunard liner.
Curly over, twirly over, over on the railings
   Early from the ferry dirling over Mersey water.
Mary Brett

AFTER FORTY YEARS

Let us walk round: the night is dark but fine,
And from the fo'c's'le we shall surely see
The lights of steamers passing to the sea,
And all the city lamp-light, line on line.

There on the flood the trampled trackways shine
With lasting gleamings shaken constantly:
The River is the thing it used to be
Unchanged, unlike those merry mates of mine.

This is the very deck, the wind that blows
Whines in the self-same rigging: surely soon
Eight bells will strike, and to his fading tune
Will come the supper-call from Wally Blair:
And then alive, from all the graves none knows,
Will come the boys we knew, the boys we were.

John Masefield

Note: John Masefield (1878 - 1967), Poet Laureate (appointed 1930), had a strong affection for the Mersey, where he trained as a cadet on HMS Conway.

Birkenhead
to
New Brighton

MERSEY FERRIES

Across the busy Mersey
    from Woodside to Pier Head
Ran the black hulled river ferries
    with the funnels black and red.
Every morning of the weekday
    at the ferry terminus
Came the groups of office workers
    off a double decker bus.
Tickets purchased at the kiosk
    Daily Post beneath the arm
They would scurry down the gangway
    hoping for a voyage calm.
Down would go the access walkway
    with a loud resounding crash.
Gates would open with a rattle,
    all aboard without a splash!
Some would join the panelled saloon
    for a comfortable ride,
Most would promenade the top deck
    with an anticlockwise stride.
Hooter sounding, ropes all cast off
    and the boiler building steam,
Speeding up the triple engine
    with the brightwork which would gleam.
In and out of ships at anchor
    funnels red and buff and blue,
Waiting for the docks to open
    to discharge their cargoes to.
Dropping speed so very slowly
    up along the landing stage,
Where the liners used to tie up
    in a not so distant age.
In would come the Seacombe ferry
    from the far New Brighton pier
Tying up alongside tugboats
    with the powerful towing gear.
Now the ferry's just a venue
    on the river tourist run
Mersey railways and car tunnels
    make the travelling much less fun.

Philip Bastow

NORTH-END GIRLS (1950s)

Freedom was a companion of North-end girls –
who lived in welcoming dwellings roundabout
                    St. James Church,
Dockers' daughters with too many siblings to count.

Wide-eyed mentors . . . stripping naked to bath in kitchen sinks,
teasing those with lowered eyes and gentle blushing cheeks.
Beginning a revolution in figure-hugging tops
                    and long straight skirts.
Sultry Ava Gardenias, look-alike Doris Days;

imaginary lovers, film and rock stars.
Sending letters of wicked passion to young men at sea,
and earning a living checking other people's dreams.
New Brighton was the playground for these rebels in black bras,

whizzing round on carousels, eyeing boys in dodgem cars.
Playing for prizes with winning darts.
Gin and laughter on the menu in the local bars,
giving friendly banter to the strict landlords.

Living in wild abandonment to big band sounds –
North-end girls, with big warm hearts,
who walked right into the Sixties . . . on three inch stiletto-heels.

Anne Green

THE ROUNDABOUT CHURCH (ST JAMES)

In Rome they've got Basilicas, in France they've Notre Dame,
In China, they've got a wall that is very, very long.
In Egypt, some pyramids grand; in Turin a Holy Shroud.
But in Birkenhead they've got a church in the middle of the road.

People come from far and near, to see this oddly sight.
It causes traffic jams and tail-backs, and angry drivers sigh.
It might just be a landmark though of course I could be wrong:
But I've never seen it open or heard an evensong.
I wonder who designed it, what chaos its erection caused.
Was it some post-modern architect, or a priest who liked fast cars?
But its presence is amazing and so I write this ode
To a rather odd-shaped church in the middle of the road.

Denise O'Shea

BIDSTON WINDMILL

Grey bonneted
sturdy in storms,
the windmill
challenges the changing years,
rooted in rock.

Once, farmers
trudged steep rocky paths
through heather and gorse
to grind their wheat
for daily bread.

Now, latticed sails,
that gaily whirled
to the music and the dance
of the wind,
lie pinioned and still.

Many a breezy trick they'd played,
once hooked a donkey by its panniers
and swung it high and left it
braying out its outrage
to the skies.

And in a savage mood
crushed a floury miller
as he took his evening stroll
and flung him lifeless
to the rocks below.

Today sight-seers
climb the hills, cross the gorse,
queue, snake heather tracks,
pay tribute
to forgotten farmers.

Infused with fresh life,
the windmill
flaunts fixed top sails,
signs V for Victory
on Wirral's sky-line.

Jean Stanbury

BIDSTON HILL, BIDSTON MOSS

When I was a child, under shadow of Bidston Hill,
We would enter Bidston Moss,
Via the stile, by the old cottage.
There a wild old woman would rant at us,
"Nothing good will ever come from this place
The Hill has a spirit,
A great dark shape with searchlights for eyes.
Will-o-the-wisps will draw you from the path
To where Jenny Greenteeth will tangle you in weeds
And drag you to her den."
We would race away,
Fishing nets over childhood's optimistic shoulders,
Across the whale-jawbone bridge
To Spraggs pond, miasmic, teeming
With stickleback, frogs, Great-crested newt.
Then the Moss became a passive victim
Drained of the dark oily blood of its waters, its turf flayed,
Overlain by the motorway's brutalist curves
Leaving only the shadows of its history;
The strange morris-men carvings
Folk memories of lost children,
Of the fatal combats between murderous wreckers
And grim excise-men, in sandstone tunnels beneath our feet;
Of wartime aircrash sites, where
Goggle-skulled pilots, six feet down, still strapped to their seats,
Await the Moss's dark guardians' return.

Graeme Kenna

BULRUSHES (BIDSTON MOSS)

My father got them for me
sometimes: bulrushes,
green-speared reed-mace
from Bidston Moss.

Leaves slender ribbons
suppling around tall stems,
topped with brown velvet
and rat's spike,

they made solid the pond's edge,
massed spears bristling against the green
of the flyover's grassed side.

In a vase, lush
and feathered with grasses
they stood high,
leaves slowly drying
green dessicating to brown,
cracking with age: dying,
but still retaining
soft brown pride.

Now far away
in a city-sprawl, my bulrushes
can still scent the season, taste
the rhythm of Bidston Moss:

a secret message makes a sudden surge,
bursts brown velvet
with tawny clouds:
soft seed corona
billowing to Bidston's breeze.

I take the old to the river
to throw their fruit windwards,
wishing there were more
to age gracefully for me,
and fluff their seeds

reminding me of my mother's hair.

Gill Cheseldine

THE ROSE HEDGE (FENDER VALLEY)

From a Fender Valley garden, Bidston Ridge
Squirms in heat-haze like a broken back,
The green of its wooded flanks
Bitten brown with sun.

In the garden, bees hum towards evening
Working the open throats of a rose hedge,
Its flowers pink-parched with drought.
Spined leaves scratch and rustle each other.

The bees leave, humming, for the hive.
Collected pollen bulges
Like shopping bags
From under buzzing wings.

The stereos falter. Silence
Is clattered with kitchen sounds;
Plates, cutlery clinking
Behind open windows.

Clouds build with stealth,
Brooding the skies. The garden,
Sick with sun, shivers its grasses,
Whispers the breeze.

The sky breaks with static. Dogs bark,
Surprised. The rose hedge stirs, its leaves
Cracking like scorched parchment,
Its throats gaping wide for the rain.

Gill Cheseldine

WRECKERS AND SMUGGLERS

Wallasey for wreckers,
Poulton for trees,
Liscard for honest men,
And Seacombe for thieves.
Anon

Traditional Rhyme

God bless Father, God bless Mother
And God send us a wreck before morning.

Old Wallasey Prayer

All ye that are weary come in and take rest,
Our eggs and our ham they are of the best,
Our ale and our porter are likewise the same
Step in if you please and give 'em a name.

Mother Redcap

POINTERS TO THE PAST

Magazine Lane, Magazine Brow,
old street names by the Mersey
evoke Wirral's past
when gunpowder offloaded
from incoming ships was stored
in magazines beneath the earth.

Houses appear clamped between
remaining sandstone walls and
turretted arch of one-time Battery.
The round house was the watchman's dwelling.
Multi-chimneyed family homes, now flats,
grand-balconied and gardened
overlook the river; sullied spray
lashes the peopled, doggy promenade.

Top-hatted gentlemen from horse-drawn cabs
once graced bay windows of *The Magazine*.
The Pilot Boat catered for the artisans,
tobacco-reeked, spittoons on sawdust floor.

The doorway arch alone remains of *Mother Redcap's Inn*
the inn was once a smuggler's haunt
with hiding places in stair-well and chimney breast.
This site is now the Redcap Nursing Home
for aged innocents; a grey haired, grey-clad lady
waves a papery white hand,
and I wave back.

Fay Eagle

CHILDHOOD MEMORY
OF SEACOMBE TO NEW BRIGHTON

Rocked by the ferry, bumped at the shore
crowding the gangway, people outpour.

Scuttling commuters, competing for spaces,
make for the turnstile with work-a-day faces.

Piling in people then panting for more,
tall yellow buses fill up to the door.

Mixed groups of children with 'jam-buttie' fingers,
race from the gangway as ferry boat lingers.

Seagulls are screeching in anticipation;
children responding with joyous elation.

Jumping and skipping, leap-frogging the bollards,
tall, fat and short ones, all 'two penny scholars'.

Promenade vagrants, from now until seven,
stretched out before them a vista of Heaven.

Colour-filled gardens slope down to the river;
fishermen waiting their live-bait aquiver.

'Stop-me-and-buy-one', the tricycled vendor,
busy supplying ice-cream to each spender.

Redundancy's landmark at Egremont Ferry,
ghosts of sad sailors some sad and some merry.

Freak waves are splashing cold spray on hot faces.
Salt air re-charges the slowing down paces.

Into Vale Park with a local band playing,
what's left of the picnic, is hunger allaying.

Then off to the Fair Ground, few pennies at ready,
'Ghosts-trains' and 'Dodg'ems', the prospects are heady.

Short time for watching the slot machine punters,
win eggs filled with secrets for souvenir hunters.

The Pier at New Brighton is walked on with wonder;
scared peeps between deck gaps as Mersey waves thunder.

The crowd and the pierrots, the lighthouse, the sand
big sisters, small brothers clutch hot sticky hands.

The ferry boat's engine throbs deep in the bone
one last wave to Wirral, then sailing for home.

Antoinette Loftus

OVER THE WATER

Looking from Crosby beach it was magic,
day-out land of childhood,
hovering pinnacles, dome, sharps and flats
of Wirral sky-line across the slate-grey Mersey.

It tempted our teenage years.
Amusements, swimming pool, ballroom, boys.
We'd take the train and ferry, giggle freedom.
But when, on New Brighton prom, we crouched
cupping a flame to light that first cigarette,
I had to peep over the parapet, to check,
convinced my Dad armed with binoculars,
would somehow be patrolling the opposite shore.

Hilary Tinsley

NEW BRIGHTON, FEBRUARY

From this car park, we know
a new angle on the Liverpool skyline.

Windows steam up, greasy.
We eat fish and chips with our fingers,

throw scraps to be caught in mid air
by hungry, spiralling gulls.

The heater toasts our feet.
Kisses are vinegar, salt and ecstasy.

Love will never know
a more intense moment.

Alison Chisholm

NEW BRIGHTON FORESHORE IN WINTER

Her face an ice-mask, she follows the tide,
upholstered against a moist, searching wind;
splashes through the random debris of the sea,
dog in pointless pursuit of wading birds,
immune to their shrill defiance.
A vision of pied beauty alive against the gloom.
They rise in anger, complain, circle and return.
Shapeless, mud-spattered hybrid thinks again
and scampers off for new quarry.

A single angler trawls for worms in the sludge:
squirming, sightless aliens,
fit only for snaring hapless flounders.

In the unkempt garden, eager shoots break the soil
heralding an explosion of spring colour.
Waiting for the grey pallor to pass.

Robin Thomas

THE TOWER GROUNDS

A broad stretch of grass
curves steeply down to the river.
Trees dot about, mostly old.
Above, a playing field.
Beyond that new homes.
Dogs and owners enjoy the grass.
Occasional picnickers and lovers
spread their rugs in summer.

As children we went to the fairground there
with merry-go-rounds, music
and the Wall of Death.
Frequenting stalls with coloured lights,
shooting, ringing and throwing balls.
But the man didn't always deliver
the prize we thought we'd earned.

I suppose the 'clean-up'
made a tidier, pleasant place.
But it's a lot less lively.

Sheila Holt

THE WIRRAL SHOW (New Brighton, 2002)

Under blazing skies -
the crowds, arena, displays.
Dogs, men, motor-bikes
dive through a circle of flames.
Old warplanes bewitch our eyes.

Ceri Courtenay

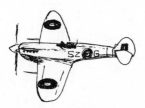

NEW BRIGHTON MILESTONES

One thousand years,
distilled,
engraved in brass,
chiselled in rock –
sandstone boulders
broadcast,
like a string of beads,
along The Promenade.

Each denotes a milestone
of the past:
invasion by the Irish Norse;
smugglers, wreckers;
builders of a sandstone fort –
(protection never needed
in the Napoleonic War).
Rock erodes to sand.

More recent yet
and hidden now
by hoardings, cinders, grass –
a fragment of mosaic
where Marie Lloyd enthralled;
a horse-shoe scar of tramlines;
the Ham and Egg Parade.
Day-trippers,
sardine-packed aboard
a 'ferry 'cross the Mersey',
pleasure-seekers cast adrift
in time.
Minutiae of our social past,
held safe till memory
is unhoused.

The moon's insistent tug
trawls oceans in her wake.
Upon the beach,
kids frolic in the surf,
undying love's proclaimed –
scored with a razor shell.

Soon, lovers' names
will be erased, moats flooded,
towers fall.
The imprint of a paw
fills up. Sand remains,
unmarked,
until the turn of the tide.

Millions of years,
condensed,
in granite blocks
amassed along
the marine wall –
a muster
against the battering tide.
Water scours,
lays bare a history
petrified in braille.
My fingers trace the record
of your day.

Jan Curran

ATHERTON STREET, NEW BRIGHTON

To Rock Point at the mouth of the Mersey
An Everton merchant came
With vision for a new Brighton
James Atherton was his name.

For years but few people had lived there
In cottages down on the strand
Fishermen drying and mending nets
Hauling their boats up the sand.

James Atherton looked to the heath-land,
He foresaw grand villas there
Four square in brick and in sandstone
Not just castles in the air.

A smart new suburb for the rich,
Merchants, ship owning gentry
Who from lofty windows could watch
Their ships standing in from sea.

He bought those high windy acres:
From craggy top looked down,
He started New Brighton ferry
So workers could cross to town.

He fulfilled his dream and it prospered
With landing stage and new pier
Visitors filled theatres and ballrooms
From places both far and near.

The rolling miles of golden sands
Lungs for breathless Liverpool
Gave Northerners their holidays;
Breaks from work or school.

Vale Park, Floral Pavilion
Winter Gardens, Tivoli,
Brought joy to many thousands
On days out beside the sea.

Climb the hill from New Brighton Station
After your day's work is done.
Remember the far-seeing founder
In the street that is called Atherton.

Tom Alsop

THE RED NOSES

Red sandstone cliffs
above a shore
where debris meets old caves.
Secret places, leading from the tide.
The haunt of moonlight men,
a tendril maze of dripping walls,
– then Mother Redcap's store.
Brandy and tobacco casks,
exotic names burned into staves,
while Jim Bowes' bones
hang golden, in the sun.

At The Hall – replete,
the gentlemen retire,
for a brandy and a smoke.
The wives silk dressed, refined,
share a genteel joke,
while Jim Bowes' bones
move slowly, in the wind.

The windchange caught the Dutchman square,
and the Dutchman missed the buoy
and Jim Bowes' men were waiting,
prepared to risk their all,
while Jim Bowes' bones
hung loosely, in their chains.

Bill Heap

DODGE CITY, NEW BRIGHTON

This is a Wild West town,
a kind of forgotten frontier,
facing the cold Irish sea
not always bravely, and the Mersey,

with its long, pained memory –
the street named for Victoria
looks like Main Street, Dodge City,
you expect people to hitch up

glorious quarterhorses, and spit,
which they sometimes do. Also,
they tend to leave half-finished
takeaways on pavements like tables,

that's life in Dodge.
Every corner has its own saloon.
Beyond lies childhood,
crabbing along the marine lake,

eyeing small craft blading across
the pond, almost level with the water,
wrestling the Mersey blast.
Total, unwilling recall knows exactly

how much it matters.
Crabs have to grab the bait, come up
like puppets dangling from grey strings.
Dodge must survive, against the odds.

Aileen La Tourette (U.S.A.)

NEW BRIGHTON GHOSTS

Standing by the red-stone, toy-town fort,
once more short-trousered, summer-sandalled,
I watch the ghosts of world-wide ships
queue up to navigate the Crosby bank.
I watch the *Ben-my-Cree*
(long melted down for patio barbecues)
steaming out to Mona's Isle.
I watch *St Seiriol and St Tudno*,
yellow-funnelled,
churning the sea of Reckitt's blue to foam,
day-trip laden, bound for Wales.

Landward, ghosts of buildings,
sad café fronts, blank-boarded,
await the demolition ball,
where once, pre-Hitler's war,
mothers ordered pots of tea
on oilcloth tables,
sneaked illicit sandwiches
from ample shopping bags
for hungry city sparrows.

The ballroom's gone
where once Bill Gregson played
and lovers danced to big-band tunes,
pre-Beatles days.
Gone is the fairground,
long gone Handley's one-legged diver,
the pier where I saw Lobby Lud,
and failed to claim the ten-pound prize.

Gone is the landing-stage,
where families disgorged in thousands
from *Royal Daffodil*,
bucket-and-spaded,
under a railway-poster sky.
Gone the swimming baths,
another car-park in its place,
haunted by gulls,
ghosts of long-legged Fifties' beauty queens.

Albert Morgan

New Brighton
to
West Kirby

NEW BRIGHTON WINDOW

Boats glide between triangles of roof-tile
that interrupt the Mersey's grey sleepwalk
from where I sit watching scows, barges, ferries
skate across the slates, negotiate the chimney-pots,

slide down the crisscross pathways hemmed
with gaudy drifts of salt and bubble that fold
back into the river's thin, grey cloud-broth
as if they'd never been. Maybe they haven't,

but something about these momentary ladders
without rungs, or with so many rungs
at crazy angles you could never count them,
let alone climb up unless you were the moon,

– the way they repeat without monotony,
sculpting the same relief maps over and over,
ruffling the river the wrong way between aisles
decked with wash, convinces me they mean

at least as much as everynight dreams,
which also leave their ladders propped
on water, as if something escapes or elopes
before they go. Tiny sailboats wobble in a line

across a rope ladder that's also a bridge.
The tips of their sails brush the roofs,
whisk between the chimneys like dusters,
as they jerk by. Then the bridge isn't.

Aileen La Tourette (U.S.A.)

DERBY BATHS, NEW BRIGHTON 1949

We struggled through a turnstile and a dingy pale green door,
Then paddled to the changing room across a flooded floor.
Each cubicle had half a door and narrow wooden seat.
The scribbled information on the walls I can't repeat.

My costume then was woollen in a shade of navy blue.
Discovering it was moth-eaten and skin was peeping through,
I bunched it up and folded it in layers around my tum,
Then stepped out of the cubicle displaying half my bum.

I realised then I had no choice, I had to jump straight in.
The green and murky water was soon lapping round my chin.
My soft and woolly costume when it hit the icy pool
Changed shape and length and sagged a lot. I looked an utter fool.

I tried to tread the water clinging tightly to the bar,
But breathless, cold and petrified I couldn't travel far.
I glanced up at the diving board, a lad was balanced there.
He dived into the water and his trunks flew through the air.

Like a group of crazed piranhas other girls and one large boy
Snatched his pathetic garment and used it as a toy.
My hands were white, my skin pale blue, I gasped a lot for air
I couldn't swim, I hated it, what was I doing there?

At last I heard a whistle: it was time for us to dress:
I staggered up the poolside, steps a wretched dripping mess.
The half door closed behind me, but of course it had no lock.
I trod on something splodgy – a discarded blackened sock.

I pressed my back against the door so no one could get in,
But slipped of course against the seat and badly grazed my shin.
Shivering, I grabbed my towel desperate to get dried.
I found the task impossible however hard I tried.

With vest stuck tight half up my back, my frock and knickers soaking,
The water in my ears and throat convinced me I was choking.
I dropped my socks, my towel fell off, my efforts were in vain.
I determined from that moment I would never go again.

Margot Hoerty

MOCKBEGGAR

Where horses of Mannanan whitely grazed
On weed-girt wilderness of shoaling sand,
Above dark hostile shore a beacon blazed
To pilot doubting helmsman safe to land.
When, wrapped in salt-wet mantle, ships lay still
And empty eyes were brimmed with rising dread,
Hoarse boom of klaxon muffled ears would fill,
Dull echoes marking time with sounding lead.
Besieged no longer by the raging swell,
Forsaken monarch, impotent, uncrowned
By time and man, this hollow limewashed shell,
Maintaining faith with mariners long drowned,
St. Elmo's halo bears on storm-racked night
As phantom keepers tend the phantom light.

Brian Mitchell

STAYING AT LEASOWE

Stark lines define a castle
where ordinary streets become
a swathe to cross the stray.
But this facade
does not front
an echoing hall, old portraits.

We race the wind,
find warmth in Axminster,
follow the porter to our room
of mirrored wardrobes, TV,
a bathroom moulded in the turret's niche.

Cocktais and menus mellow evening
anticipating prawns and flambéed steak.
Alone but for the waiter, we touch hands
and feed each other strawberries.

Night is lush
with glimmer of street lamps,
white light from stars.
We lie awake
afraid of sleep dividing us.

Egg and bacon sizzle
to dissipate night's magic.
Spell released, we talk
about the Sunday market
and the tunnel home.

But Visa cards and cases can't dispel
impressions of a castle's romance,
a whispered swish of skirts,
ghost shimmer on the stair.

Alison Chisholm

BANKING ON MORETON CROSS

Side by side
Standing solid
Symbols of the City
Black Horse and Griffin
Looking down their noses
Across the floral tributes
Which glorify the Cross
In a kaleidoscope of colour
Rivals
On a modern battlefield
Of gyrating ceaseless traffic
Noisy and smelly
halted but briefly
As the Pelican calls a truce
While ragged armies cross
And recross
In confusion
And yet
Within the confines
Of two banking halls
Order
Figures in neat ranks
All black .
Red banished
Cashiers slotted in allotted places
behind the barricades
Managers lost in manager's rooms
Securing service
Selling services
To the ragged army
Of complaining
And complaisant customers
Grist to the mill
In the granaries of Profit
And Loss

Gordon Thompson

OVERCHURCH

Under the drab concrete, deep in the soft earth
lie my childhood pleasures.
Red brick boxes press on the ghosts of hedgerow
where fragile violets, blue and white, taught me
If you don't look, you don't see.

Four-wheeled destroyers sit neatly parked on tarmac
beneath which was once a watery treasure-trove.
Here the great horses cooled feathered fetlocks
among the matching bull-rushes or yellow flags.
Metallic dragon-flies gyroscoped, pausing
only to curve tubed tails beneath the surface.

Who remembers now the green tunnel
that was the path to Greasby, arched trees
and the hazels and brambles, thick and snatching.
Once there was a man, flat-capped
'doing something naughty'.
Only Maureen Mawson protested as we fled.

Now, children ride bikes along the street
or play on miniscule manicured lawns.
Not for them the joy of seeing the fields change
from the soft lavender of mayflowers
to the shining simplicity of buttercups, shoulder high.
Then the tawny-purple of the flowering grass-heads
soon to be toppled for winter feed.

Are computer-games and Mickey Mouse holidays
sufficient recompense?

Gina Southern

ARROWE PARK

The lovers' myrtle bloomed in ages dark
Before the roving Vikings brought the plough –
And did their children play in Arwe Park?

The slave ships' human cargo disembarked
Their degradation Arrowe did endow
The lovers' myrtle bloomed in ages dark.

'Elizabethan' Hall, a proud landmark
A tribute to the Shaws, but whisper how –
And did their children play in Arrowe Park?

Fifty thousand lads, a jolly fine lark
Until rain made their camp into a slough
Where lovers' myrtle bloomed in ages dark.

Young soldiers training learned their choice was stark
'Kill or be killed, they're alien boy scouts now'.
And did their children play in Arrowe Park?

As parents stroll they may perhaps remark
Despite the tears and heartache yet somehow
The lovers' myrtle bloomed in ages dark
And still their children play in Arrowe Park.

Angela Keaton

Note: *Vikings (*Vikingr; *a sea rover or pirate) brought the plough
to Britain. ARWE in Celtic means a ploughed field. The Shaw
family who built Arrowe Hall were slave traders and it has been
speculated that slaves were used as labour to build the Hall and
landscape the park. The World Scout jamboree was held in
Arrowe Park in 1929. Gunners were stationed in the Park during
the Second World War and did their training there.*

THE GREASBY PUMP

The gentle breeze whispers softly of the past –
Children used to gather to play at the pump,
grown-ups in the corner talked of their jobs,
sweethearts though speechless giggled all the way,
mothers sought advice on how to bring up a child.

The underground spring is eager to narrate –
The water was fetched by people at this place
for quenching their thirst, cooking their meals,
washing their clothes and watering their fields.
Here gossips were exchanged, thus news travelled fast.

Old maps hidden away are restless to point out –
The pond has been known for long to exist.
In Harry Hopps' painting at Williamson Art Gallery
the pump during days of its glory is seen –
a source of water for near-by residents.

Birds on trees sing day after day –
When the running water came, there was no need
for the pond, the pump, the trough and the well,
they were forgotten under layers of the rubbish.
Where is the crowd now? To whom shall we sing?

Many happenings of Greasby had happened at the pump,
though neglected for years it's now restored
that memories of the past may live on forever –
those footsteps, chattering and laughter of people,
those clinking buckets, the gurgling pump!

The gentle breeze whispers softly of the past . . .
the underground spring is eager to narrate . . .
old maps hidden away are restless to point out . . .
birds on trees sing day after day . . .
Many happenings of Greasby had happened at the pump!

Amitav Ghosh

Note: *The Greasby pump was stolen in the year 2001.*

ROMANS IN IRBY

A keen wind slices
the trenches we have dug.
The sky's grey March shower-cloud hovers
over our brown box of soil,
lies level over a blue expanse
paling down towards the sea,
taking the orb of light with it to the west,
as urns of oil and salt were carried
by trade to this point where we dig.

Golden glints of chipped burnt clay
and dun daub and Roman orangey wares
in tiny blister-burst fragments are revealed
by trowel, spade and mattock;
the blunt thud as sandstone sears,
scrapes against the metal blades.

We're standing on a Roman level,
having trowelled back layers of time;
its context dotted with clues of pottery,
slag, iron workings, haematite, hearths,
heat-fractured stones, bits of black ash –
all a mosaic emerging.
The post-holes; craters,
empty silences posing larger questions,
deeply shadowed in the afternoon light.
I stand and ponder over one,
let my thoughts fall into the fill:
it's negative; texture gritty loam,
soil colour-coded, cut, dried,
labelled, drawn, scaled, noted.

A cobble-like dwarf wall, a pit,
and beam slots slice across the other trench,
its stone-packed post-holes like tiny wells;
secret shrines. The Roman contours disappear
under a modern concrete path, find
their own way under the neat gardens.
This watery ditch and bank
kept animals palisaded:

a cow-shed's uncovered –
these farmer's tilled with Roman methods
on Iron Age ores; and flints turn up
in flurries too, to tell their tales.

From this hill, down through centuries,
eyes looked on emerald woods,
descending to Celtic seas;
looked out to beacons
blazing on Welsh hill-forts.

Romans in Irby
smelling salt from the tides,
recalled Mediterranean brines.
I dig deeper, trowel back the earth
like a wave retreating on a shore;
and tap into deeper soils:
gouge out the base of a pot –
another find, a landmark, proof:
the Romans lived in Irby.

Ceri Courtenay

Note: *Excavations were carried out in the early 1990s by Liverpool University archaeologists on the site of a Roman farmstead/villa.*

GEORGE CONGREVE,
FIRST VICAR OF FRANKBY, DECIDES ON HIS FUTURE
AS A COWLEY FATHER: c.1871

I have tried to teach them here,
through painted glass and images,
that beauty is a window through to God;
and preached against the heresy
of nature as a siren to be shunned.

Close linked to this peninsula
by family, but Irish born and bred,
I learned with Celtic saints
to contemplate God's love,
as here, in vivid sandstone rocks,
the small wild rose, the honeysuckle
and geranium; the butterfly,
the blackbird on the lawn,
the lark soaring on the common;
the badger, fox and viper in the grass.
And even faced with cries of pain,
my spirit sighs with mad Ophelia,
'Rosemary for remembrance . . .
pansies for thought . . .' which speak,
as truly as the bread and wine,
of flesh once broken, rising,
still ascendant, in this strip of land.

But having walked the sands to Hilbre,
that small island in the estuary,
its silence loud with migratory birds;
caught by the tide, I have sat
and realised this triple paradox:
that to be free, I must be under
strict obedience; to heal estrangement,
be estranged; to be at one
with all that lives, be set apart.

Alan Gaunt

STRANGER GOD

On the Saughall Massie lane
The entire landscape appeared to be
Worn out,
Weary of winter and mankind.

Hedgerows and fields
Lay lifeless
Beside the dull grey track.
It was as if the Earth,
Forsaken by the sun,
had grown cold
And lacked the will to carry on.

Not a breath of wind
Stirred the naked branches,
Damp and dripping with moisture,
Trees rotted before their sap could rise.

That day,
The plough would have broken
In the iron-bound furrow
As seed germs
Of crops and grasses
Expired in the fossilised darkness
Of an alienated soil,
Crying out
For the wild swirling dance of Light.

John Curry

DOVE POINT, MEOLS

Sometimes, winter gales
storming the coast
find,
beneath shifting sands,
stumps of oak and ash
where once a Roman Legion camped.
Sometimes a coin,
Nerva or Constantine.

Sometimes, north winds
striding the waves
sing,
through flying spume,
wild airs the Roman Legion sang
before the altar stone
of Mithros or Jupiter.

Sometimes, through sea mist,
sandalled feet
that knew the seven hills
seem near,
near . . .

Dora Kennedy

THE SUBMERGED FOREST, MEOLS, 1636

But greater wonder calls me hence: ye deepe
Low spongie mosses yet remembrance keepe
Of Noah's flood: on numbers infinite
Of fir trees swaines doe in their cesses light;
And in summe places, when ye sea doth bate
Down from ye shoare, 'tis wonder to relate
How many thousands of theis trees now stand
Black broken on their rootes, which once drie land
Did cover, whence turfs Neptune yeelds to show
He did not always to theis borders flow.

Richard James
*(*from *Iter Lancastrense)*

from: HOYLE LAKE, 1794

Dear scene! that stretch'd between the silver arms
Of Deva and of Mersey, meets the main
And, when the sun-gilt day illumes its charms,
Boasts of peculiar grace, nor boasts in vain.

Though near the beach, dark Helbrie's lonely isle
Reposes sullen in the wat'ry way
Hears round her rocks the tides, returning, boil.
And o'er her dusky sandals dash their spray.

Mark to the left, romantic Cambria's coast,
Her curtain'd mountains rising o'er the floods.
While seas on Orm's beak'd promontory burst,
Blue Deva swells her mirror to the woods.

If to thy quiet harbour, gentle Hoyle,
The shattered navy through the tempest flies,
Each joyous mariner forgets his toil,
And carols to the vainly angry skies.

How gay the scene, when Spring's fair mornings break,
Or Summer-noons illume the grassy mound,
When anchor'd navies crowd the peopled lake,
Or deck the distant ocean's skiey bound.

Like leafless forests, on its verge extreme,
Rise the tall masts, or spreading wide their sails,
Silvering and shining in the solar beam,
Stand on that last blue line, and court the gales.

The peopled lake, of song and lively cheer,
And boatswain's whistle bears the joyful sound,
While rosy pennants, floating on the air,
Tinge the soft seas of glass that sleep around . . .

Anna Seward

OUR GRENDEL

There must have been something else but sea.
I try to remember the school, the church, the people

but the sea was the real professional – the rest
an amateur production. However vast the cast

the sea went one better, put on an epic,
a clincher. No need to go and check its

credentials. Trading under a host of disguises
the parent company was easily recognised.

The council built a groyne, a wall, iron-railed
and then, in autumn, all else failing

sent for the sandbags. We lived, I suppose
as the Geats with Grendel. Our sandy homes

full of Chinese chests and shrunken skulls,
restless with women and empty of sons.

Grandfathers outside the pubs with salt white hair
sat on in uniform and stared out there.

Diana Hendry

BIRTHSTONE

Along the midnight silvered, watery way,
The three-quartered moon
Reflects the eastern dawn.
Starshine moments
Lap in the wavelets
Playing with salted stones,
Dance greenly upon delicate Mya shells.

Beyond the lighthouse and the Hoyle Bank
Waves boom,
Pound upon half-tide rocks
Which resist the sea swell,
And drown mermaids' locks
Along with curlew cries.

Here in the cold, dark light
Of morning,
We witness a new year dawning,
Anticipate the golden sun
With our warmth
Which melts the hoar frost
At our feet,
Leading us towards
Those Summer moments
When sail-boats
Are glued
To the surface
Of a windless lake.

John Curry

THE GHOSTLY PROMENADE

Remember
the Bandstand in the gardens,
where nearer to the ground then
we could smell the lush flowers growing;
where Mothers pushed babies in high prams,
and people could take tea on white-clothed tables
and stir it with Apostle Spoons.

Remember the local fishermen at Sandhey Slip
discharging 'the catch' from Nobbies:
and the fish sellers – Ethel, Nellie, Weetie –
and the wind, blowing away May Hughes' voice as she cried –

Nice Hoylake Flukes, try them while the bacon's salty.

Remember drinking on endless Summer days
from the Victorian Fountain, chipping our teeth
as we giggled and pushed
for some of its rusty-tasting water.

Remember the Paddling Pool
where we dipped our feet
and tucked skirts into knickers;
and sailed home-made boats
tied to bits of string.

And the Swimming Pool
where we swam in all weathers,
and drank hot Bovril in the Café,
and posed glamorously (we thought)
by the two, too-cold cascading fountains.

Jacqui Baker

OUT OF BOUNDS

Royal Liverpool Golf Club at Hoylake, Wirral

The sky is bright today;
high cloud thins and separates
like cells. A wind from the east
flaps the flags on the greens:
the sound of whips cracking.

Sturdy in red
a golfer trudges the fairway
lugs his caddie-cart of woods
and irons. With no margin for error
he has overshot, sent the ball out of bounds
beyond the low turf wall of the seventh.

I too am out of bounds;
a trespasser among bunkers
and screening trees
slipping past The Stand
– the old parade ring, with echoes
of silks and saddling bells –
skirting the edge of the links
crossing in reverse order
the Royal seventeenth
Lake, Field and Rushes
to reach the dunes.

Now wind lifts my hair
ruffles the waters in the estuary.
The safe-path to Little Eye
comes back in the slow turn of the tide.
I am hoping for the sight of Redwings
Field-fares, Siskin and Snow-Bunting
and maybe, as night comes on, the croak
of Natterjacks calling from the slack
of the marsh around Red Rocks.

Jacqueline Bartlett

FORCE 8

Warnings of gales came
when I was driving home to warmth.
The maroon gun propelled my cat
underneath the bed, made me run
to watch the lifeboat leap the waves
and pray for those in danger
– child, yachtsman, tourist
who's misjudged the tide –
and for the crew, friends who
over years have rescued strangers.

Closing curtains against spray-lashed glass,
I exclude weather, but all evening
wonder if distant searchers
battle still, not knowing
as they trough through cliffs of water
if this launch will be successful,
whether all will come home tonight.

I am one with those silent gatherings
at slipways, huddled against fear,
staring into mist, listening
for voices on the tide, tired
triumphant tones that tell of lives saved,
or, when the engine dies, a silent
coming in, wading ashore, Coxswain
slowly seeking one young wife
who reads the message in his eyes.

Peggy Poole

Note: *The Royal National Lifeboat Institution has stations at
Hoylake, West Kirby and New Brighton.*

WINTER WIRRAL TWILIGHT

Befogged and bleared
by a day of small, close things,
I stretch and yawn and turn my head away
from cluttered papers and the peevish ring
of phones, and look outside.

Beneath my window, deep
in a gorge of dusk, a glimmering, shifting
snake of home-time cars creeps,
winking topaz eyes, following the swift
lilac river out of the city.

Far Welsh hills
simmer in shadow, their mulberry mass
distilled by evening's alchemy to a vast,
translucent haze of amethyst air,
cradling a new-born moon.

Then, leaping high,
the brilliant, breathless diamond of the sky –
an arching ice-jewel, rare
and subtly tinted.

Over the sea,
Venus, thrilling the turquoise West
like a white-hot pearl,
burns alone.

I gaze and breathe,
filling my eyes and lungs with crystal;
then turn
to answer the phone.

Tracy Smith

TO WINIFRED ON HILBRE

You did not see me above you
on the ridge, passing you by
intent on my own purpose
at the island's end: to sit

alone like you, watching
the sea and clouds seeming
to fuse on the horizon
but in essence always one.

When I returned you saw me
smiled and when I reached you
asked me why I shook my head
and laughed. I was your cloud

riding the wind above you
unsuperior, secured
in the certainty of clouds:
always to their sea returning.

Alan Gaunt

see Pg 11.

A PLEASANT PLACE TO LIVE

A finger of land points out toward the sea,
Close confined by two broad rivers that fold
In tight embrace a store of quiet delights;
Rocky slopes clad in royal purple and gold
Of heath and gorse; sandy woodland tracks
Gently meandering through aisles of silver birch;
And age-old cliffs that guard the windy shore
Loud with sea-birds' cries.

The sands of Dee stretch wide, splashed with pools
Left by the ebbing tide, and mirrored there
The fiery rose and gold of splendid sunsets,
Lovelier far than any Turner painted.
Then the slow dusk, and the chains of light hang twinkling
In the bases of the hills. Beyond them lie lush valleys,
The spreading fields and frowning peaks of Wales,
Land of the singing speech.

Elsie Williams

INDEX OF POETS AND ILLUSTRATORS

Alsop, Tom, 130
Anon, 14, 16, 70, 79, 93, 99, 122
Baker, Jacqui, 40, 152
Baldock, Carole, 19, 26
Bartlett, Jacqueline, 153
Bastow, Philip, 24, 75, 116
Bennett, Martin, 38
Bennett, Miriam, 36, 111
Bower, Fred, 37
Bradley, Linda, 28, 81
Brassey, Jane, 39
Berry, John, 55
Brett, Mary, 30, 90, 113

Callery, Dymphna, 18
Carr, Valerie M., 60
Craggs, Susan, 21
Cheseldine, Gill, 121, 122
Chisholm, Alison, 126, 139
Chisholm, Malcolm, 102, 110
Coles, Gladys Mary, 11, 15, 17,
    22, 63, 86, 95, 107
Coles, Lindsay, 34
Cordon, Muriel, 56
Corfe, J.M., 26
Courtenay, Ceri, 49, 51, 127, 144
Crompton, Richard, 74
Curry, John, 16, 147, 151
Cusick, Edmund, 87

Davis, Alan, 72
Dennison, Marjorie, 65
Dhenin, Kathleen, 109
Eagle, Fay, 123
Gaunt, Alan, 146, 156
Ghosh, Amitav, 143
Gilpin, R.J., 74
Green, Anne, 103, 117
Green, Geraldine, 54
Griffiths, Douglas, 52, 92
Halligan, Gus, 112

Hanson, I.H., 93
Hartley, Joan, 64
Heap, Bill, 132
Hendry, Diana, 150
Hikins, Sylvia, 57
Hodges, Betty, 49
Hodgson, Mary, 29, 53
Hoerty, Margot, 137
Holt, Sheila, 127
Home, Lorna, 47
Hope Allen, Barbara, 91

Jackson, Kit, 37
James, Richard, 148
Jamieson, Norma, 33
Jones, Bettina, 59
Keaton, Angela, 142
Kenna, Graeme, 120
Kennedy, Dora, 12, 45, 48, 148
Kingsley, Charles, 66
Kirby, Sandra, 68, 104
Lamount, Dora, 108
Lancelyn Green, Roger, 77
La Tourette, Aileen, 133, 136
Leigh, Egerton, 83
Lewis, Jean, 89, 106
Lloyd, Edward, 69, 94
Llwyd, Richard, 42
Loftus, Antoinette, 124

McLean, Don, 106
Martin, Sue, 71
Masefield, John, 12, 114
Milton, John, 44
Minter, Patricia, 38
Mitchell, Brian, 138
Morgan, Albert, 134
O'Shea, Denise, 118
Parry, Sheila, 85
Plested, Laura, 82
Poole, Peggy, 20, 105, 154

Priest, Frank Jocelyn, 28
Pride, John, 41, 46
Rankin, Freda, 35, 48
Reynolds, John, 76, 83, 108
Riley, Gina, 88
Roscoe, William, 96
Seward, Anna, 149
Slater, the Rev FG, 70
Smith, Tracy, 155
Southern, Gina, 141
Stanbury, Alan, 109
Stanbury, Jean, 62, 97, 98, 119
Sumner, John E.M., 113
Thomas, Robin, 84, 126
Thompson, Gordon, 80, 140
Tinsley, Hilary, 112, 125
Tolkien, J.R. (trans), 14
Walton, Peter, 65

Whitby, Thomas, 96
White, Mary, 27, 31
Williams, Elsie, 157
Wilson, Heather, 78, 101
Withers, Bruce, 25

Illustrations

Lindsay Coles, 13, 15, 30, 32, 34, 36, 43, 48, 54, 61, 73, 100, 115, 135, 157

Gladys Mary Coles, 14, 82

Howard Coles, 23, 41, 67, 86, 102, 104, 110, 114, 115, 118, 127, 129, 131, 138, 150

Ceri Courtenay, 16, 21, 50, 65

ACKNOWLEDGEMENTS

I am grateful to Guy Huntington for permission to reproduce one of his very fine photographs on the front cover of this book, and to Kenneth Burnley, founding editor of *The Wirral Journal*, for his kind interest in this project. I also wish to thank Guy Huntington and Kenneth Burnley for the immense pleasure and stimulation given by their books of photographs and prose, *Images of Wirral* and *Seasons of Wirral* (Silver Birch Press).

My warm thanks to all the poets who have contributed their work; and particular thanks, for editorial assistance, to Jacqueline Bartlett, Kit Jackson and Jacqui Baker. I am grateful to Lindsay Coles, Howard Coles and Ceri Courtenay for the illustrations.

I extend thanks for the generous encouragement of Iain Corlett (Linghams Booksellers), Helen Bower (Hammicks Booksellers, Birkenhead), Rob Smith (Metropolitan Borough of Wirral), John Baxter (Birkenhead Central Library), and Angela Heslop (BBC Radio Merseyside).

For the use of copyright material grateful acknowledgement is made to:

the Estate of John Masefield for an extract from 'A Masque of Liverpool', and 'After Forty Years'; the Estate of Roger Lancelyn Green for 'Poulton' from *Poulton Lancelyn* (1948); the Estate of J.R.Tolkien for the extract from *Sir Gawain and the Green Knight*, translation, (Allen & Unwin, 1978); Gladys Mary Coles for 'From Hilbre Island' from *Liverpool Folio* (Duckworth, 1984), 'Wet Spring Bank Holiday, Dee Estuary' and 'Takers' from *The Glass Island* (Duckworth, 1992), 'The Scapegoat'. 'For the Centenary of Wilfred Owen' and 'The Black Chair Of Birkenhead' from *The Echoing Green* (Flambard 2001); Alan Gaunt for 'To Winifred on Hilbre' from *Always to their Sea* (Headland, 1982); Diana Hendry for 'Our Grendel', previously published as a *Mandeville Broadsheet*, (1976); Peggy Poole for 'Tell's Tower' and 'Force 8' from *Trusting the Rainbow* (Brentham Press.1994); Heather Wilson for 'The Ghost of Poulton Hall' and 'Morpeth Dock' from *Wirral Visions* (Metropolitan Borough of Wirral, 1982).

Special thanks are due to all the poets who, at my request, wrote poems for this anthology: if any of these pieces have since appeared elsewhere, due acknowledgement is made to the editors and publications concerned.

A number of poems in this anthology have been heard on BBC Radio Merseyside and BBC Network North West.